OREGON BASKETBALL

A SEASON OF FIRSTS

A behind the scenes look at the road to a
championship and beyond...

OREGON BASKETBALL

A SEASON OF FIRSTS

A behind the scenes look at the road to a
championship and beyond...

BEN LINDQUIST
Forward by Coach Ernie Kent

Photos by Eric Evans
Cover Design by Bright Ideas Graphic Design

Published by Jepsen Publishing
ISBN 0-9724428-1-2

First Printing, January 2003
Printed in the United States of America
Cover design by Bright Ideas Graphic Design
All Photos by Eric Evans Photography

Printed by IP/KOKE in Eugene, Oregon

This book is dedicated to the 2001-02 Oregon Basketball Team.

B. L.

ACKNOWLEDGMENTS

I wish to express many thanks to my teammates, coaches, family and friends. Hopefully this book will be evidence of the positive impact you've all provided in my life. My Love goes to my Wife, Joy, although I always wondered if I could write this book, she always supported me and never doubted! Thank you! To my Mom and Dad, Dian and Bunk your belief in me has produced so much more than the following pages, thanks for never letting me give up!

CONTENTS

FOREWORD

In the 29 years I have been associated with college basketball, I have come to realize basketball is the ultimate team game. There is something magical about those teams that play in perfect harmony once they have surrendered themselves totally to the "team first" concept. However, in our society today it is difficult to find those teams, because athletes are far too focused on themselves. It is that "me first" mentality that has destroyed the team chemistry of so many potentially great teams. It has cost them the reward of a great season and also cost several coaches each year as they have lost their jobs.

What you are about to read is the behind scenes journey of a great chemistry team that for this season, in this moment surrender themselves to each other and have a mystical and magical season that will forever change their lives and the community that supported them.

As a father, head coach, community leader, or business person, we all often wonder how to get our families, i.e. "teams" on the same page, and if they are getting the message that will give them an opportunity to be successful.

As the author of this book, Ben Lindquist, former player at the University of Oregon, received the message and has done a masterful job of putting that message into words as he captures our championship season in the following chapters. Ben will take you into the depths of our program explaining the heart and soul it takes for a team to come together at this level of play.

Along the way you will feel the passion and the emotions of failure and success and the road traveled to get there. This book is a testament to what it takes for teams today to understand the compassion and sacrifice one has to have and make in order for your family, team or business to be successful.

I hope you will be touched as much as I have been, to have a member of your family grow and realize through his own heart the magic of the message that has been passed on to him.

INTRODUCTION

When something magical happens you want to share it with others. I could think of no other way to share this magic, than to weave my deep love for the game of basketball and the story of an historic season that reached beyond the realms of just success into the following pages.

In writing this book I was reminded time and time again about what made this one season so memorable, unlikely, and so special. There is always a great deal of pleasure that comes from personal success, but for our team overcoming adversity and reaching our goals together provided more than a sense of accomplishment, it provided an understanding of what a group can accomplish together. A knowledge that will prove more meaningful and valuable than any ring, trophy or accolade in each of our lives.

It is my goal that by the time the final page is turned, you the reader will feel that this is more than the story of a basketball season. More and more each day I realize that the ingredients that helped create our spectacular year are occurring less and less. Whether you are a high school athlete, parent, coach or business owner, I have tried to bring life to the ability of leadership, sacrifice, selflessness, and determination, when each is truly applied to the framework of a team.

CHAPTER 1
The Beginning of a Journey

"You cannot create experience. You must undergo it." — *Albert Camus*

March 11, 2001. We were all waiting for the phone call, the call from Director of Basketball Operations Mark Hudson informing us of our bid, not to the NCAA tournament, but instead to the NIT. As badly as the season played out, we all wanted a chance at any form of postseason play. The phone never rang. Finally I called Coach Hudson, and it was over just like that. My mind quickly raced over the past year wondering how it happened, how a team with so much talent could end up the way we did.

It's a funny feeling when a season ends. Some guys are relieved; others disappointed. However, there is always one question that is universal — how is the season already over? For our particular team it was more than that. It was, how could the season already be over? And how did everything go wrong down the stretch? How could we have been 10-1 only to end up at .500, pulling out a late victory over civil war rival Oregon State just to finish at a disappointing 14-14?

What had started as a season with so much potential, a chance to build on a previous year's third place PAC-10 finish and an NCAA tournament bid, had instead finished as a painful exhibit of poor teamwork and self-destruction.

Each player and coach plays out the season in their minds a hundred times over, wondering how they had let something that had started so well slip away. Seniors reflect on a year of disappointment and try to draw on some positive part for the future, knowing that the real world's wait is over. Returning players do the opposite, they take those feelings of disappointment and use them as motivation for the spring, summer, and most importantly the upcoming season.

For every team the road to success is a journey, and every journey has a beginning, for our team March 11, 2001 was the end of one journey and the beginning of another.

There is a lot of heartache after a season; feelings of failure can be compounded quickly. It is not hard for a team to carry the lingering effects of a bad season into the spring and summer. To the coaches it made no sense to drag out an already disappointing season any longer. So from that day on all the talk was about the future, and deservedly so, we had a great core of returning players. That nucleus included not only seniors-to-be, but young guys who now had a year of major college basketball under their belts. And, with the addition of a deceivingly good recruiting class, the future was indeed worth looking to.

Part of looking to the future is having some form of closure. For those of us who had played, the annual team banquet was just the closure we needed. It was interesting showing up at the banquet and noticing about 100 fewer people in attendance than the previous year's banquet. That group had hailed the previous season's NCAA tournament appearance and a third-place conference record that was a school high (13-5) at the time.

This year was drastically different than the previous, and the effects carried over into that evening's event. Not a great deal of emotion was involved, and it certainly felt like something was missing. The majority of us quietly wanted the banquet to be finished before it started. The general feeling of the team members was 'put the past in the past and focus on the potentially bright future.'

The night was pretty uneventful, coaches spoke, awards were handed out, highlight videos shown, and players gave their farewell speeches. However, as good as it felt to have the year finished; it was truly a joyless feeling sending off four seniors the way we did. It was something, which triggered silent promises to myself that whatever it took I would not finish my career in the same manner. Before we realized it, the night was over and the season was officially finished.

The following week was right back to business. And when I say business, it was just that; not one person wanted the same result as the last season. In fact guys like Luke Ridnour, Luke Jackson, and Freddie Jones made it known that as long as they were at Oregon there would never be a season like the last.

At one point, after another late season loss, Ridnour was on his way out the locker room door when he was greeted by Coach Ernie Kent's wife. Without hesitation he said, " I will never let this happen to this program again." In a year that had been full of empty promises, this promise seemed to be more than just comforting words to a coach's wife.

The world is full of people that talk the talk, but seldom do you find people who walk the walk. That spring and summer we all knew in order to be successful we had to walk the walk. Part of doing that was the grunt work, the monotonous, sometimes boring or exhausting work. Four days a week in the spring, we woke up at 7 a.m. and lifted. The coaches knew if we were going to get better and make a run at the end of the season, that we would not only need to be in better shape, but physically stronger than we had been the previous year.

Finding motivation for this time of the year was not difficult; however, it was tough to get back into the swing of three workouts a day after a long grueling season that seemed to never end. It's strange how the better the season goes the shorter it seems to last. Unfortunately it also works the other way around. Within about three weeks after the season we were back into playing every day while continuing our weightlifting and individual workouts.

The coaches wanted to make sure that within all the workouts and lifting we didn't get burned out. Part of breaking the monotony was scheduling some team activities…

SOFTBALL EVENT

On one particular day the coaches scheduled a coaches vs. players softball game at the women's softball field in place of individual drills. The game also included a home run derby beforehand.

Both players and coaches were pretty excited for the game, every player on the team relished any form of competition, and this would be no different.

Everyone arrived a little early to take some batting practice. Because of a lack of players, the coaches invited Joe Giansanti, a local TV guy, and Pastor Keith Jenkins, the team chaplain, to try and fill the holes. Before play started, there was a lot of trash talking; it became clear early on that the coaches were taking the game more seriously than we were.

Activities started with the Home Run Derby, which only featured players. Each player got 10 outs with anything that didn't clear the fence considered an out. There was definitely some laughing going on when a bunch of basketball players tried to hit a softball as hard as they could. A few guys went to the ground trying to swing so hard. Of course I wasn't one of those guys.

The first round went pretty fast; I think I probably hit two home runs, and wouldn't be moving on to the second round. My M. Jacobs Furniture summer softball team would've been very disappointed, I never could figure out why I wasn't invited back for a second season.

A few guys had some baseball experience and they did pretty well. Then there were the guys who used pure strength, namely Freddie. The semifinals came down to Luke Jackson, Freddie, Mark Michaelis and James Davis. Mark appeared to be the early sleeper, but Luke also hit some towering balls onto the supply shed behind the outfield fence. After five outs only Freddie and Mark remained.

In the finals everyone thought Freddie would win. He had crushed the ball farther than anyone else in the previous rounds. However, Mark went first and after dropping five home runs over the outfield fence looked in control.

Freddie came up to bat and struggled from the start, picking up two quick outs on ground balls. He got going a little bit but picked up two more outs along the way. By the time he got to his final out Freddie was tied with Mark for the lead.

He took a few seconds to gather himself, switched sides of the plate and looked as though he planned to hit left-handed. This, of course, got everyone riled up, I think we thought he was only joking and would switch back after playing to the small crowd. However he did no such thing. Now things had gotten interesting.

We all thought Freddie was going to swing and miss, or, if nothing else, ground out. As the first pitch came he did nothing, standing there as though the pitches came any differently from the machine positioned on the mound, again playing to the crowd of teammates, coaches, and passersby. The second pitch came and, with an emphatic WHUMP!!!, Freddie sent the pitch over the right field wall, clearing the fence by a good 15 feet.

As unimportant as the team home run derby might be, we all stood amazed. Maybe a solid hit into the outfield, but a home run left-handed, for crying out loud? We knew Freddie was athletic but nobody gets up and hits a home run right-handed, and then decides to switch to his left like a curious super-hero testing his newfound powers. Again even though it was a meaningless contest, that home run seemed to amaze everyone at the field, everyone except Freddie, that is.

After a few minutes we decided to move on to the actual game, knowing that the only thing more dramatic would be to have "Shoe-less Joe Jackson" stumble in from a corn-lined outfield.

First the coaches batted. They jumped on us right away, scoring four runs in the first few innings. What had seemed like an easy victory had turned into a must-win come-from-behind situation.

However, after getting the score close, our lack of any real baseball experience caught up with us. At one point we had Chris Christoffersen get a hit and run to third base instead of first, obviously because of his baseball-free upbringing in Denmark.

By the end of the game Coach Graham had hit two home runs and the coaches had embarrassed us. Fortunately for us there were burgers and hot dogs waiting so the sting of defeat was short-lived.

Along with weights and pick-up basketball, we had also started individual workouts. This is where the NCAA allows the coaches to work with the players for two hours a week. In the fall we end up focusing more on defense and going through some of the plays with the new players. But, in the spring this usually consists of some conditioning and offensive work.

The NCAA is very strict about enforcing just about every rule it has. For us, Coach Kent took everything involving the NCAA quite seriously, and for good reason. If the NCAA finds you in violation and punishes you, the damage can ruin a program for years. It can also ruin a coach's career.

If there is one thing I learned at the Division I level, it's that the NCAA has a rule for everything. For example, recently Jason Kapono had a great quote after playing at Arizona State in a game where the fans threw everything from pizza to spare change onto the floor. In regards to the spare change he said, "I would have picked it up but it was probably an NCAA violation."

The spring was filled with intense workouts, and with summer approaching, we all looked forward to a little spare time, or so we thought. We had a meeting about halfway through the spring. The minute we walked into the meeting you could tell that the coaches had something up their sleeves.

"Everyone will be staying for the summer" Coach Kent said. I didn't really mind because I had a rental agreement and a wife, but the look on some of the guys' faces was evidence that they had their own plans, which, as of that moment had changed. After some description of what he had in mind, coach's plan made more sense. He wanted everyone, including the recruits, to not only be in Eugene for two months of the summer, but also wanted us to take some classes. That was clearly a tool to help get the new recruits adjusted to college academics. The reasoning behind the summer stay was that the NCAA had just passed a rule that lets the school pay for not only returning players' school and housing, but also the following years recruits, something which hadn't been allowed until then. More importantly Coach wanted us to spend time together, get to know each other and push each other every day to get better on the court.

THE SUMMER

The summer is probably the easiest time to have slippage in things like conditioning, motivation and work ethic. A lot of times guys will go home, hang out with old friends and unintentionally get out of shape, occasionally getting to the gym to put up a few shots. A lot of guys will even sit all summer, playing pick-up once a week, then wait until a couple weeks before they get back to campus and start getting back into a routine. These were exactly the things that Coach wanted to guard against.

Freddie scoring in transition against UCLA

Something Coach thought would help us to become a closer team was to have us participate in a weekly activity. The idea seemed a little cheesy, in fact some of the guys probably didn't want to do it at all. We would go to people's apartments and hang out and play video games. Then we started going to movies. However, finding a movie 15 guys want to see is pretty difficult.

Bowling was the next experience. Similar to softball it certainly brought out the competitive nature in some of us. I was quite surprised by a few guys who looked as though they had been bowling more than just a few times with their families or a girlfriend. We even had a few team meals over at my apartment. My wife Joy offered to cook and did a great job, but after a few meals, feeding 6-8 guys at a time gets a little expensive.

It was apparent team members were, if nothing else, getting to know each other off the court, and quickly building common ground. One of the final things we did as a team was float down the Willamette River in truck tire tubes. Coach probably wouldn't have been too happy if he had found out about this especially since a few guys didn't even bring tubes. Of all the things we did, this was probably the most enjoyable. I never thought that we would be able to get all the guys to go, especially Freddie, who openly admits to hating water. In fact, I thought the whole thing would never work out. Along the way we ran out of gas somewhere in Springfield, and then Kristian got pulled over because Luke Jackson and I had our tubes hanging out the windows while we were driving. However, we ended up making it down without any injuries or near-drownings.

A few months later Sports Illustrated came out with the issue that had Joey Harrington on the cover. I was flipping through the pages one day and there was a big spread of the guys on the football team floating down the river together. I got a good laugh out of seeing that. Apparently there is some winning magic in the waters of the Willamette River.

MIDNIGHT BASKETBALL

That summer Rid, Jay, Jackson, and James had moved into a four-bedroom house about five blocks down 18th street from Mac Court. They had previously lived over by Autzen Stadium, and felt they not only wanted to be closer to campus, but especially Mac Court. Coming in the door their freshman year all four of these guys were gym rats, especially Luke and Luke. They could sit in the gym and work on their game all day. After up-and-down years for the four of them, they saw the summer as an excellent chance to improve their personal games.

Along with shooting, lifting, and playing pick-up with the other guys, Rid, Jay, Jackson, and James would meet about 9 or 10 in the evening at Mac Court, and play two-on-two until midnight or 1 in the morning.

Now, getting into Mac Court during the day is not a difficult task. However, late at night, it is all but impossible. There is a door at the back of our locker room that is hardly ever used, and occasionally guys would prop it open if they wanted to come back that night and get some shooting in. Mac Court as a building is usually closed in the summer around 6 or 7 p.m., and that's strictly enforced.

So just about every night the guys would prop the door open with athletic tape, which actually worked pretty good. The teams were always the same, Rid and Jay against Luke Jackson and James. The games were to 11, make it, take it, and usually they would play a best-of-seven series.

"They were always heated battles with a lot of trash-talking" Rid later said. Rid and Jay also claim that they lost only a few times, usually forcing James and Jackson into an argument with their use of the pick-and-roll. However, Luke J. and James would probably tell a different story.

Part of sneaking into Mac Court, was dealing with the issue of lighting. The lights in Mac are on timers. There have been countless times when we would be playing, working out, or even practicing and the lights would go out. This wouldn't be much of a problem except the lights take about 20 minutes to warm up and turn back on. However, there are a few lights that stay on all the time. These lights provide just enough illumination for players to function, but not enough to feel comfortable. There were a few times that we had been playing pick-up and the last game was interrupted with the lights turning off, this of course drew "looks like I shot the lights out" from whoever had taken the last shot. Nevertheless, we always finished.

When the foursome played late at night, the lights were always dimmed. However, after a few evenings this was no longer a distraction, but instead an accepted part of their midnight basketball.

Along with the games came the music. James would bring his stereo and plug it into the floor just off of center court. The music of choice? Classic rock of course. That same stereo was later used occasionally in some fall pick-up games, until one fateful afternoon.

The jack that the stereo plugs into sits about six inches into the floor. There is a little wood cover that runs flush with the floor so nobody trips on the outlet.

During pick-up games the losing team usually sits just off the court where the stereo happened to be that day. Chris's team had lost the first game and he was sitting on the sideline waiting for the next game to finish. When it concluded, he got up and trotted onto the court. All of the sudden the sound of a door slamming caught everyone's attention. The music that had been playing loudly, suddenly stopped. We all glanced over at Chris and got a glimpse of not only smoke coming from the box in the floor, but also a few seconds of sparks. The stereo cord had been severed by Chris's size 18 shoes. The funniest part about the whole thing was that Chris had no idea what had happened. He looked around sort of lost, shrugged his shoulders, and walked on to the court ready to play the next game. James took a few minutes to inspect the stereo, not quite sure what to think, but after assurances the stereo could be fixed, the pick-up games went on.

By the end of the summer we had accomplished a number of things as a team that were unrelated to actually playing basketball. We had grown together as a team. The thing with growing anything is it takes time. You don't plant a seed and water it, then walk out the next day and find a bright flower in its place. It takes time. Sometimes it's impossible to even see the growth at all. For the summer our team was no different. There were times when we all wondered what we were doing there. After all, we spent the majority of the year together anyway.

But, by the end of the summer we were closer not as basketball players, but as friends. It took more than just our summer; it took a willingness on each player's part. It was another one of those things where I didn't realize the effect it had until much later.

The more I look back, the more I realize that each time we gave something as a team, or individually, we were rewarded tenfold. There is a quote by Phil Jackson that relates the game of basketball to life. He says, "inside the lines of the court the mystery of life gets played out night after night."

As silly as it sounds, this couldn't be more true. Yes, it is still a game, but the things that you learn, endure, sacrifice, and strive for can be closely related to life's important lessons. That summer a number of teams took advantage of the NCAA rule change, spending the summer together growing as basketball players. However, I doubt many of those teams grew the way we did that summer — as friends.

In addition to becoming a closer team in the summer, we improved as basketball players. Coach Kent always said that, "the summer was the time where you put the work in." It's the time you work on your confidence. Then, when the season rolls around, he will build on that confidence. I always felt that Coach Kent was a fair coach. He not only clearly explained what he expected of his players, but also gave every player a chance to earn his minutes on the floor. He made it no secret that the summer was the time to earn your minutes for the upcoming year. I don't think there was a guy who didn't get better over the summer. The unfortunate thing about every sport is that only a certain number of guys can play at the same time.

Occasionally I would relate playing time to the Top 25 rankings that are released every week during the season. On all the sports shows, the hosts and guests would regularly talk about which team they thought should not only be in the top 25, but sometimes in the top 10. The funny thing is that not once did they mention who should be taken out of the top 25 to make room for these other teams that they felt were being overlooked.

I constantly remember talking to the television, hopelessly trying to convince them that there are only 25 spots in the Top 25. These guys regularly talk as though there are 35 spots. This is very similar to basketball. Every player wants to play and start, and, if they don't, they don't understand why. I took the approach that there are only five starters, and that, if I was going to start I would have to be a better player.

If I wasn't able to be one of the five best players, then I would find a way to get onto the court. Did everyone have the physical ability of Freddie? No, but as a player it's important not to compare yourself to another player. This can only do you harm. I felt that I needed to be the best that I could be, and if that wasn't good enough, or perhaps someone at the time was shooting the ball better, or playing better defense, then I could live with that. Like other guys on the team, I was concerned not about who was going to start or play the most minutes, but instead about doing everything I could to get better as a player.

That summer we all got better in one way or another. By the end something was different about our team. "I was excited, I felt coming out of the summer we had something nobody in the nation knew about, not even Eugene," Luke Ridnour later said in reflection. With the summer over and players heading back home to take a short break before the start of fall classes, our confidence and our team had indeed grown. We all felt that we were at the beginning of something special, not really aware that the something special had been started months earlier.

CHAPTER 2
Back to School

"There can only be one state of mind as you approach any profound test; total concentration, a spirit of togetherness, and strength." — Pat Riley

Coming back to school is never easy. It always seems like the summer is too short. For the guys who are from out of state, the short time at home goes by too fast. However, as short as the break seemed because of the time spent over the summer, it felt good to have any form of a break.

We always play the Sunday before the first day of school and then have a meeting right after at Mac Court. Usually introductions take place and Coach Kent gives his first big speech, we get a pair of shoes for working out, then discuss class and workout schedules.

The only guy that couldn't make it for the summer was Ian, so there was still some introducing going on, but other than that everyone else quickly got reacquainted. There is a certain feeling of excitement and nervousness when everyone gets back. It's similar to the first day of school as a kid. One thing that stood out from the beginning was how well everyone got along. From the start you could tell that we were going to have a fun year. There were no real cliques or certain groups that only hung out with certain people as there had been in the previous years.

The meeting was a long one. You could tell that Coach Kent had put a lot into the preparation and it was apparent that he had expectations he wanted this team to meet. Coach Kent made it clear that he would not let what had happened the year before happen again. We were going to have to work and the players that didn't want to work wouldn't play. One thing that is vital to any player's success with Coach Kent is being on the same page he is on. If you're not on the same page he is on, then in reality you're not on the same page as the team. Each year that part started to make more and more sense. Probably the best thing about Coach Kent is that his door is always open, I'll never forget talking to a friend who played at Colorado State. He used to tell me that the only times he spoke to the coach off the floor was in semiannual player-coach meetings at the beginning and the end of each year.

I never really went into Coach Kent's office and met with him on a formal basis, but many times just went in to talk about non-basketball stuff. That was the way it was with all the coaches, the players were able to have personal relationships off the floor, something that is not very common at this level.

COACH LITZ

We had heard that over the summer Fred Litzenberger would be joining the coaching staff. He was coming over from the woman's team after the resignation of Jody Runge. I don't know how excited we were at the time; every guy on the team could share a time they waited outside the gym waiting for the women's practice to conclude and heard a fiery man yelling and blowing his whistle. Before we got to know him I think we all thought he was a little crazy, but the best part is he would probably tell you he is.

One of our first individual drills of the fall he brought out these full-length mirrors with a line taped through the middle. When I first saw the mirrors, I thought it was a joke, I'd never seen anything like it. In an attempt to help the player not only get accustomed to being in a defensive stance, but also to condition the body to stay in that stance, he propped the mirrors up and had the players sit parallel to the mirrors for a few minutes at a time. Not only was Litz getting a kick out of the whole thing, but the other coaches seemed to enjoy it too. I've heard coaches claim they had won games using smoke and mirrors and after our little experience with the mirrors I was left wondering one thing… where was the smoke?

"We wondered a little about his techniques, especially the mirrors. We thought it didn't matter how you played "D" as long as you got it done" Rid and Jay Anderson later mentioned. However, after about a couple of weeks he had quickly become everyone's favorite coach, and the things he said made more and more sense.

To understand Litz you have to know that he yells, and is pretty intense when he does it. However, you also have to understand that he not only knows what he is talking about, but won't try to embarrass anybody.

I soon realized that yelling was how he communicated in practice. It was not the Bobby Knight type of yelling, but more of the professor in a huge auditorium making sure the people in the back could hear. The thing that stood out the most to me throughout the year was that not once did he use a curse word on the court or off. In a day and age where coaches are known to have some of the foulest mouths, along comes a guy who, with all his emotion and yelling, didn't once have to use a curse word. Probably the most impressive thing was that he never wanted to take credit for any of the success we had on the defensive end; he was just happy to be apart of it. He knew what it took to win, and doing what it took to win seemed to be what he enjoyed the most.

Often times people will refuse to address certain problems faced, and even more often people refuse to ask someone else for help. However, Coach Kent knew that our defense struggled, and we needed someone who would focus 100 percent of his energy on making us a better defensive basketball team. Coach Kent brought Litz in with the idea of making corrections to a defense that was last in about every statistical category in the conference. To prepare, Litz watched hours of game tape and compiled about 50 pages of things we needed to fix.

The Defensive Guru...LITZ!

Sure enough, everyday in practice Coach Kent turned 20-plus minutes over to Litz to work solely on what he wanted to do defensively. I think every guy would tell you that this was their worst part of practice. It was certainly the toughest part...... every time we looked up at the scoreboard and saw 20:00 everyone looked at one another and gave one of those, "here we go" looks. It seemed like a couple of times the clock never moved.

I thought that by the end of the year we would slowly get away from that part of practice, but every day at some point Coach Kent turned the time over to Litz and every day he gave everything he had. I was always impressed with how we never got away from emphasizing defense every day, certainly something that contributed to the turnaround from the previous year.

There were a few times I thought Litz was going to yell so much he would keel over, in fact he warned us before the year that he was diabetic and if his blood-sugar got too low he might behave a little strangely. As for his age, no one ever figured out how old he is. One time I asked and he said he was 200 — the funny thing was, he said it seriously.

Along with being a great coach, he was a great friend to every guy on the team. He always treated everyone the same, no matter if you started or never saw the floor. He had a joke or a saying for every situation you could imagine. Out of all the funny guys we had on the team he was one of the funniest.

There is a period of time between school and practice starting, that is filled with individual workouts, lifting and pick-up basketball games. There is a lot of role identifying during this time. Players are trying to show the improvement they have made over the summer. Meanwhile the new players are just trying to figure out where they fit in and prove that they belong. The individual workouts are probably the most dreaded, especially when Coach Litz would start off by saying, "go ahead and put the balls down; we won't be needing them until the end."

It seemed like three weeks before we even shot the ball in the individual drills, the focus was on improving individual and team defense. The best thing about Coach Litz was that he could yell and scream, but after the workout he was the first guy to say, "hey, you did a great job today, why don't we look at some film to see what you can improve on?"

Although this was the most dreaded part of the week, it was probably the most beneficial. Not only did we work twice as hard as we had done the previous year, but we got a lot better defensively in all areas.

As I mentioned earlier, strength was an important area for our team, and we knew we would have to be stronger than we were the previous year. Everyone had gotten not only tougher, but physically stronger, many of the guys putting on 5-10 lbs of muscle. I think anybody would tell you that we worked harder in the weight room in the spring and summer than during any other year. And the best part was, it showed. Workouts consisted of hour-and-a-half four-day a week workouts. Each workout forced you to push yourself. In the previous years guys would just try and get done as fast as possible, skipping some lifts or not doing the full weight. This year it was different though, guys were challenging themselves each week to get stronger.

The usual week looked like this:
Monday :
8:00 –12:00 Class
1:00-2:30 weights
3:30-5:00 pick-up / or individuals
7:00-9:00 study hall
Tuesday :
8:00 –12:00 Class
1:00-2:30 weights
3:30-5:00 pick-up / or individuals
7:00-9:00 study hall

Wednesday:
8:00 –12:00 Class
3:30-5:00 pick-up / or individuals
7:00-9:00 study hall
Thursday :
8:00 –12:00 Class
1:00-2:30 weights
3:30-5:00 pick-up / or individuals
7:00-9:00 study hall
Friday:
8:00-12:00 class
1:00-2:30 weights
Afternoon Off!!!

The pick-up games at this time of the year were usually sloppy, hardly ever representing game-like play or situations. However, it was a great tool for not only conditioning but also helping players to get a better feel for other players' styles and tendencies. Not to mention the games also provided some healthy competition at a time in the year were you can't wait to get the season going. It is difficult at this point in the year to determine how good the team could be, pick-up games are so different from a regular college game. In the college game each possession is important, in a regular pick-up game at the rec center or at Mac Court, the only really important possession is for game point.

Probably the hardest part for the student-athlete is the student part. It's hard for people to understand the sacrifice that goes into playing a college sport. Carrying a full class schedule and then spending the rest of the day either lifting, running, or doing individual or other team workouts is not an easy feat. For a person who doesn't understand time management, school can be a real challenge, especially given the schedules we maintain. Playing the game we love is the easy part, not just because of the many rewards, but because, for our team, we all grew up with the dreams of playing at a high level and all that comes with those childhood dreams. Growing up, kids don't say, "one hour left, final exam, it's just me and the essay question, I write left to right and get a 100 percent on the final and an A+ in the class." When kids are growing up, they dream of having the game on the line and hitting the big shot. I wouldn't necessarily say that this is a bad thing, but that it's reality. However, it is a shame if a kid doesn't come to school and get a free degree. As difficult as it gets for some student-athletes, it seems to be like anything else in life, including basketball, if you put the time and effort into it, you can be successful. I will be just as proud of my various academic achievements as I am with those from basketball.

School is no longer the type of place where a student-athlete can just show up and pass the class. The days when teachers give athletes special treatment are past. Now some students are at a disadvantage because teachers occasionally believe societal stereotypes about student-athletes. I have been very fortunate to get some of what I feel are the best teachers at the university, but I have occasionally had a teacher who didn't like athletes at all. Coming out of high school, athletes are usually at a disadvantage because of an easy road through high school because of mild forms of special treatment. Unfortunately the college level is sometimes a shock to incoming players. This was something that coaches and counselors are always concerned about.

One of the ways that coaches try and avoid academic difficulty is by requiring students who get below a 3.0 GPA to attend mandatory study hall for eight hours a week. I was on it for my first term and vowed I would never go back. My first year that requirement wasn't enforced as strictly as it is now. If you don't get your eight hours in a week, coaches have what is called a strike policy. If you get more than three strikes during a term, you lose tickets to the next game. I'm sure there were times when family or friends showed up and didn't have a ticket because players had their tickets taken away. This same policy applied to missing class or a tutor appointment. I have found that university officials are making an honest effort to try and rid themselves of the stereotype of special treatment for athletes.

THE DR. CARR EXPERIENCE

"There comes that mysterious meeting in life when someone
acknowledges who we are and what we can be, igniting
the circuits of our highest potential" — Rusty Berkus

Each year the team goes to what Coach Kent calls "the Retreat." The retreat takes place about two or three weeks into the fall term. The idea behind the retreat is to help the team get closer, to identify potential problems that teams go through and to decide how we will handle them when they occur.

Also the retreat is a chance for the players to bond, not as teammates necessarily, but instead as a family. The reason for this is that when you develop a family-like relationship you have something that is consistent on and off the court.

When you throw so many different personalities and backgrounds together, disagreements happen, especially when you have to be with the same 15 guys for 10 months out of the year. However, by getting to know each player on a personal level, you begin to care more about them as a person than as a basketball player.

This is the purpose of the retreat, to help each player not only get to know his teammates, but to understand more about who they are as a person. Each year Coach Kent has been here they have gone up to the United States Basketball Academy, which is just up the Mackenzie River. The idea behind that is to get away from all the distractions. We had some great times; some guys had never really been up in the mountains in that type of environment. Each year coach brings in a professional who specializes in maximizing the potential of businesses and teams. There are a number of exercises, and meetings designed to help build trust, problem-solving, and teamwork. Last year we spent probably eight hours a day meeting, so this year there was an emphasis on keeping it shorter.

Part of keeping it shorter entailed staying in Eugene and holding the sessions in the team room at Mac Court. This year a man by the name of Dr. Carr was brought in. Dr. Carr had a great deal of experience in all areas of building organizations and teams and identifying their problems. He was a shorter man, who, when he spoke, always sounded like he knew what he was talking about. When he talked, everyone listened. At one point President Clinton had asked him to be the Drug Czar for the United States, without a doubt a problem area for not just our country, but also the world. Dr. Carr had also worked with a number of players and teams across the country.

The first thing he had us do was put our chairs in a circle. We all came in and sat down. He stood up in the middle of the circle and started telling certain guys to sit in certain spots. He did it with a look on his face that made it seem like he knew something we didn't. After that process was complete, introductions took place and we had begun.

Dr. Carr held a basketball in his hands and said, "this is the cake, if you do not have the cake, you cannot speak!" Then he explained how things would work, if you had something to say, then you would raise your hand and the person with the cake would throw it to you.

Simple enough, or so we thought. About halfway through the first session, I started to realize how significant the process was. So many times people carry on a conversation and just wait to get their two cents in whenever possible. After the initial curiosity of the cake wore off, and you got a feel for how the conversations would go, you stopped waiting to think about what you would say next and started to listen to what the other person had to say.

Dr. Carr directed the majority of the conversations. He would ask the questions, and, if someone wasn't paying attention, then he would put that individual on the spot and have him explain his actions.

The best part about the whole thing is that if someone replied with a maybe or a probably, he would say, " Probably? Do you mean Yes or No?" This always caught someone off guard. I never realized how often people spoke using such non-descriptive words. Part of the whole experience involved being honest. If a question was asked and the person wasn't sure about his answer, or maybe even concerned about offending somebody else, Doc would grill him until he expressed how they really felt.

"I want you to pick someone you feel you need to get to know better," Dr. Carr said. I think the majority of us thought we really knew the other guys sitting in that circle, but we couldn't have been more wrong. It was kind of funny how James and I picked each other. We weren't the best of friends, but we both thought we knew enough about the other. We split up into our groups of two and spread out all over Mac Court. Dr. Carr gave us a simple sheet of questions that we were supposed to ask and then record the questions. We were given a time limit. We were told if we exceeded that limit, we were showing disrespect for our other teammates. No one wanted to be the guy who came in a minute late, so we immediately started the question process. The questions were simple background questions about family, personal achievements, and past experiences.

After a few icebreakers, we started to share some real personal experiences. James had struggled in his first year. Just about every player comes in his first year and expects to do the same things he did in high school. It had become a frustrating topic for him, but he opened right up and shared what he had learned and how he had grown not just as a player but as a person. He told me about his family and all that he had experienced growing up. Someone I thought I knew was, within 15 minutes, someone I had never known. I never realized all that he had gone through just to get to where he was that day. I had forgotten how tough my first year was.

For the second half of the exercise, he started asking the questions, and I also shared personal experiences that guys on the team had probably never known. I think we all felt something empowering about opening up and sharing something about ourselves that only close friends and family knew. After about 45 minutes we met back down in the team room not really knowing what the next step would be.

Dr. Carr then proceeded to ask each person what they had learned about the other person. I think every person learned a great deal about his teammates, or what Dr. Carr referred to from that point on, as our family. I had never realized what guys had gone through to get where they were, I was not only surprised but, for some reason, felt closer to some of the guys who shared personal stories within those few hours than I had over an entire season.

I went home that night and told my wife that the strangest thing had happened. Within a few hours I had become good friends with James. Of all the guys on the team that I thought I would say that about, he was probably the last, not because I didn't like him or anything like that, but instead because I didn't see anything in common. However, he had many of the same struggles I had, not just with basketball, but we had both come from a home that was seriously affected by divorce.

The next day we shared what we had learned the previous day. There was a change in the mood of the team. Everyone seemed a little closer, and it felt like each player had a deeper appreciation for his teammates. I quietly wondered how many other teams would be doing something like this, and hoped that it would lead to some form of success on the floor that year. After all, we had done something similar the previous season and everything we talked about went out the window when things started to go bad. However, as I mentioned, something had changed, perhaps it was the brutal honesty or the fact that we all entrusted our teammates with something personal and important to us.

FREDDIE'S TWO-MILE RUN

In between the break from summer school and the beginning of the fall term, there was a set of criteria and tests that each player had to complete. The first was a conditioning test where each player had to complete a two-mile run in a certain time. For the guards it was 14 minutes and for the big guys it was 17 minutes. The other test was a shooting test that required the guards to make a certain amount of shots in one hour. Not only did a certain number have to be made, but they had to be made using different moves and from different spots on the floor. The idea behind both tests was to maintain the progress that we had achieved during the summer, so that the time off didn't ruin the months of hard work.

Freddie himself hated the idea of just running around the track. He was the kind of guy who would get into shape by going to the gym and playing. When the day came for everyone to run the two miles, I really thought that every guy on the team would make it. Luke Jackson had sprained his ankle earlier in the week, so he would end up running it the next week without any problems. Other than that everyone else was ready to go. A few of us had gone to the track a few days before to get a feel for where we were. Again I didn't think that there would be any problems.

After weights we all met at Hayward Field. It was perfect weather to run, sunny with no breeze. Two miles on the track is eight times around. We started the first four laps without much difficulty; everyone was pretty close together. Slowly lap-by-lap Freddie started to fall behind the group. A few of the guards had set times they wanted to reach, so after the first mile we started to pick it up. The big men were still trucking along like big men do. They were going to make it, but not in any record-shattering way. The guards didn't struggle at all, making it with a few minutes to spare. By the time we were finishing up, Freddie had come to a slow jog and it was clear he wasn't going to make it. The team members tried to push him, but his back had tightened up and he wasn't going to finish.

No one really knew what to think. We had assumed that everyone would finish and were a bit surprised when Freddie didn't. The coaches announced that he would be running the two miles again a few days later until he completed that requirement.

After that we were off to the next test unaware that we would have to complete the shooting test after not only weights, but also a two-mile run. Of course this is what the coaches had in mind. They wanted to see where the team was in its conditioning. The shooting test was pretty uneventful. Everyone finished in more than enough time.

A few days later Freddie ran the two miles and didn't finish again, this time stopping just short. At this point people started to wonder what was going on. In all honesty, I just don't think he was a good long distance runner. Some guys can run and run, but Freddie was not one of those guys. The next week he ran again, still not finishing, but getting a lot closer. By the time Dr. Carr's seminar came around, Freddie still hadn't completed the test. In one of the sessions, talk of leadership came up. Everyone in the room knew that, if we were to be any good, we had to have a consistent output from Freddie. If we were going to be great, Freddie would have to be a leader and our best player.

At this point there were a lot of doubts, not necessarily negative, but simply doubts about the direction we were headed in terms of leadership. It was clear that the team was looking for someone to follow. We all wanted to follow Freddie, but something didn't seem to fit.

Freddie had experienced three years of much-publicized underachievement. The newspaper constantly ran articles about his inconsistency, and the opponents' scouting reports were similar. There was always talk of Freddie not being able to put two good games together. It was far from the overrated talk that follows many players, Freddie was someone who had all the potential in the world, but had been tagged with words like lazy and inconsistent.

There were a few times in the sessions with Doc that the realms of brutal honesty were tested. Dr. Carr had showed us the way we needed to communicate within our new family. Along with that newfound knowledge in communication came honesty. Freddie had expressed his desire to lead the team. That's when Coach Hudson, looked like he was going to burst. When Hud spoke, he always did so with a great deal of emotion. He was the kind of guy who was frustrated with others not working hard, and, at this point he had heard enough. Talk of leadership had spilled over to commitment, and what we as players would commit to.

"Freddie, will you commit to finishing the two mile time today?" Hud said.

I was shocked; everyone was surprised, but especially curious for Freddie's reply. He replied, saying that the mile just wasn't his thing, and he couldn't promise he would make it.

A few guys, including Coach Kent, mentioned that they wanted him to commit to making the time. I glanced over and Dr. Carr was sitting with his arms folded and a look on his face that said we were finally starting to get somewhere.

Sensing the importance, Freddie agreed, and just like that we got up and headed down to Hayward Field. Everyone wanted Freddie to make it, just the idea of him failing brought questions of uncertainty regarding the team's leadership and future. He started off pacing himself. It's much harder to run a long distance by yourself than it is to run with others because it's difficult to tell if you're going too fast or too slow. To help him each time he came around, Josh, the graduate manager, would yell out his time, and the team would give words of encouragement.

Finally, with about 30 seconds to spare, Freddie crossed the finish line to the sound of applause from the team and the coaches.

Anxious to see how Dr. Carr responded, I glanced over to catch his expressions. The only way to describe how he looked was — unimpressed. Not only did he seem as though there was no question Freddie was going to make the time, but also like he had planned the whole thing, and, as far as he was concerned, this was business as usual. A few older women, who had been what looked like speed-walking also gave their applause, although I don't know if they really knew what the heck we were doing out there on the track that afternoon.

There was a certain sense of relief. In a season filled with defining moments, this was one of the earliest and most important.

It seems strange, but that two-mile run proved not only that Freddie would led us, but also that he would led us with the expectations and pressures of the team on his back.

What had happened that afternoon was more than Freddie finishing the two-mile run in the required time. After all, everyone on the team had done it and knew he could do so as well. There was a great deal of pressure on Freddie to finish the two-mile, and everyone realized it. In fact, I think we felt a little guilty that we had put him in that situation and wondered what the consequences would be if he didn't finish.

From that point on, the question of who was our leader was never asked, Luke and Luke had led by example during the summer and would continue, and now Freddie was ready to lead as a senior and our best player.

Just like something had changed over the summer and, after the first day of the retreat, another change had taken place. We had solved a problem we didn't even know we had — leadership!

LAST DAY OF THE DR. CARR EXPERIENCE

At the start of each session, we would pass the cake around and tell what we had learned the previous day. At the end of the last session, we all went to Mac Court and stood around the "O" at center court. One by one the cake was passed and we shared what we had not only learned, but what we wanted to gain from the experience. Everyone spoke about words like trust, honesty, and family. In my first two years at Oregon, I had experienced the highs and the lows not just individually, but also as a team. I shared the experience of the NCAA tournament my first year, and spoke of how even though I didn't play in the overtime loss, it was one of funnest experiences of my life. I committed that day to do whatever I needed to do for the team to be successful. If that meant me not playing another minute, then so be it, the feeling of accomplishing something together was far greater than the individual satisfaction of minutes played.

The whole week I had made comparisons to the previous years and how the retreat was beneficial until the adversity had struck. I finished by saying that this team was not like last year's team or the team before that. The most important thing to me was winning a Pac-10 championship, and, as I looked around the circle at my basketball family, there wasn't a guy who didn't have the same look on his face. Did I know that day that we were going to win a championship? Probably not. After you win one, you realize how rare they are.

So many things have to go right, oftentimes requiring some good luck. That day I might not have know what the destination would be, but I knew that the journey would be special.

THE START OF THE SEASON

At the beginning of each season there is a great deal of uncertainty for each team, regardless of what school it is or the players they have. Before the season every team talks about things like the winning their conference tournament and going to the NCAA tournament. However, by the end of the year, those things turn into a reality for some teams and hope for a better year next season for others.

Our team was no different. We had several returning players, but, beyond that, a lot of uncertainty. The forward spot was probably the area of the most concern, the previous season was filled with 30-point performances by opposing forwards. Another season like that and we would probably end up in the same place. With the addition of Robert Johnson, we had an established defender and rebounder in the junior college ranks. However, he was a bit of a question mark at not only a higher level, but in a conference full of tough forwards. Our bench was not necessarily untested, but the problem with any team is not only playing time, but also finding the right rotation, another area that had plagued us the previous season. With the addition of Coach Litz, we had a proven defensive coach, but how the team would respond to his techniques and style was another important part of the puzzle. Defense had been our biggest weakness in 00-01 and, like the other concerns, we could ill afford a repeat performance on the defensive end.

Another one of the NCAA rules is that you can only start practice on a certain day. The night before that day, we all meet in the team room, and Coach Kent explains what's called the "System." The System is all the plays, strategies, principles, and the philosophy of Coach Kent's basketball program. If you have any questions from style of play to what to pack on road trips, this meeting usually answers it. Part of explaining the system is passing out the play book, that includes, obviously the plays, but also the team philosophy and schedule from that day until the last scheduled game. This is the time where we talk about the off-the-floor requirements including, academics and representing the team in a positive manner. Also included are our offensive and defensive style of play along with the expectations from each position on the floor. Probably the most important part of the meeting is the explanation of roles on the team. The basic philosophy of Oregon basketball is centered around the idea of making the team better.

I am pretty sure a number of teams have not only similar ideas, but books that are handed out at the beginning of the year. However, I doubt that those same teams emphasize and teach those principles and philosophies from day one until the last meeting in the locker room. Every team and coaching staff talks about building a team and the whole notion of the team before any one player, but our team not only talked about it, but knew that if we were going to be successful, we would have to live by it.

"THE PLAYING LADDER"

For every incoming player the question of playing time is an important topic. This meeting was also the time to address this issue through what's called the "Playing Ladder." The Playing Ladder determines three things — one, which players not only start, but usually finish the game. Two, the 9-10 man rotation, and three, which players are the subs after that. Following the idea of a ladder, it starts from the bottom and works its way up to the top. The bottom features simple requirements like going to class and taking care of business. The next rung on the ladder is doing the extra work after practice like shooting or conditioning. The next step is who understands the "System." This is the point at which players start to distance themselves from others. The majority of players can take care of business off the court and get in some extra shooting, but understanding the "System" or what coach wants out of you individually is where it becomes more challenging. The final rungs in the ladder are the deciding factors in who gets the minutes and starts — who performs within the "System" and most importantly who performs constantly.

There really is no mystery to who Coach Kent plays. Part of the reason that we go over the "playing ladder" before we even begin practice is so that every player has not only a clear understanding of what is expected of him but what it will take for him to play.

For a player the toughest part of the season is the beginning. You put in all the time in practice, but you wait a month to play any games. Our practices were pretty uneventful, a few scrimmages here and there to try and break up the monotony. But, other than that, we were just a team trying to find ourselves within the bounds of practice.

By the time our first exhibition game came along, it had already been too long. It's always an interesting experience playing an exhibition game. You get these teams that have been traveling for three weeks playing every night, and probably don't even want to be there. Then you have this team that has been waiting for eight months to play a game. There is seldom a different result than a victory for the home team. Our team wanted to use these games to see where we were as a team and also to try and find some rotations that work well. It's strange, but certain players play better together than others. Part of the challenge as a coach is trying to find the right rotations that work together. Of all the teams I have ever played with, I don't think that I have ever seen five guys that played as well together as our five starters!

Before each exhibition game, there is a little ceremony that both teams participate in. The visiting team is announced and lines up in a straight line while the home players all sit on the bench and are introduced one player at a time. When your name is called, you are supposed to run out and hand the exhibition team's players an Oregon t-shirt or hat. In return they give you a gift from either their country or team. Last year they gave us this ridiculous poster that had every word spelled in Russian. For this particular game we received a bottle opener with some Australian logo on it, a practical item for a bar, but not a college basketball team.

My first year I was visibly nervous. After all this was my first game as a member of a Division I basketball team. I, for some reason, thought it was one of those things where you run out and throw the t-shirt or hat into the crowd. We had done something similar at my junior college and I was so nervous that I wasn't really watching what the other guys announced before me were doing, I was more worried about throwing it and hurting someone. When my name was called, I sprinted out and threw the hat to some guy in a wheelchair and ran over and shook the foreign player's hand. He kind of had this look of confusion on his face but I was so nervous that I didn't put it together; I just thought he didn't understand English. After the introductions, I headed back to the bench and Coach Graham informed me that I was supposed to give the hat to the player, I can only imagine how red my face was. At that point I'm sure not only the other team, the crowd and my own team were confused, but especially the guy in the wheelchair. The worst part was we were short a hat for the other team, and there was no way I was going to go ask the guy in the wheelchair to give the hat back. After that experience the coaches made a special effort to tell the players what to do with the items before the game.

Each of the two exhibition games were a blowout, and were never in question. However, the coaches and the players all knew that those two teams would be the worst of all the teams we would face from that point on, so it was important not to get to excited about where we were. After a regular day off, we were back to business preparing for our next challenge, a three-day, three-game tournament at home.

PREPARATION

There is a lot that goes into preparing for each opponent. Coaches go through the regular ritual of tracking down film of the other team, sometimes having an opponent's film Federal Expressed the next day. Coaches alternate the scouting report of the next team among the assistants. However, Coach Kent would always watch the game tape several times just to make sure that the scouts were accurate and also so that he was prepared. I always used to think it was funny that we had so many meetings. Then I found out that the coaches had meetings every morning for at least an hour or two. The problem with having to scout a team and come up with a game plan after watching one or two game tapes is that you don't always get a good feel for how good or, in some cases, how bad the team is. About every three or four games we would get a scouting report that would say that a certain player on the other team couldn't shoot. So in our defensive game plan we would sag off the player and play the drive over the shot. It never failed. Whenever we had this situation the player would come out and hit his first three jump shots, forcing a halftime adjustment and a few sarcastic remarks about the scouting report.

With these exceptions, we were probably one of the most well prepared teams in the nation, without, of course, going overboard.

Something a lot of coaches have a tendency to do is over-prepare a team, which results in forgetting about playing the team's own game. One of the things that helped our team the most was the fact that we were not only well-prepared, but each game we also focused on playing our game. That was our mentality down the stretch; we would make sure that we knew the other team's offensive and defensive tendencies, but our real focus was to go out and do the things that we had worked on and practiced for so many months.

Along with the numerous meetings and scouting sessions, we would have what's called a Walk-Through about two days before every game. A lot of teams do this. Our particular team would put together a scout team that usually consisted of redshirt players, thrown in with an occasional coach or manager. While we would watch film the scout team would work on the other team's plays, and then that day in practice we would go through each play a couple of times, making sure that we not only knew how to defend it, but also making sure that we could recognize the sign for the play or the offensive set that the play was run out of.

Each team has a different way of calling their plays. For our team we have hand signals and verbal calls. The coaches figured that, by the end of the year, every team knows the other team's plays. It is just a matter of the one team running them well and the other stopping them. This year we were able to run our motion offense so well that we only really ran plays out of timeouts and when we needed to settle the game down. Other teams, however, have some bizarre ways of calling plays. The weirdest is probably Stanford. The Cardinal coaches have a number or name for every play that is printed on a giant card. This is an attempt to not only inform the team of the plays when the crowd is loud, but also so that they don't have to hold up a hand signal or shout a verbal play call, thus informing the other team. I thought this was pretty cool my first year, but each year it made less and less sense. After the first time we played Stanford, we knew the terminology for all their plays, so all we had to do was look over and see what play they were running and then inform the rest of our team. Again they probably felt that it wasn't so much how the opponent defends the play as much as it is how they run it. Other teams have certain sets that they run all their plays out of. This was also a dead giveaway to the play they were running. Occasionally, we would be walking through a team's plays and say to each other, " these are pretty good plays; we should run some of these." And there were times that we did end up putting a play or two in.

Our main goal in walking through the plays was to get a feel for what the other team would run and to figure out where their points of attack were, whether it was from the post, off the screen, or just in the overall movement of the play. Probably the hardest team in the conference to prepare for was USC because the Trojans had so many plays. You would spend 45 minutes a day going through their plays. Then the game would come and they'd run only five or six of them, running each play until you stopped it. When you stopped it, the Trojans would go to another play until you stopped that one.

We would not only go through their offensive plays, but also their out-of-bounds sets, not to mention their defensive stuff, usually including a few full and half court presses combined with some zone defenses. By the end of the year you rarely see something that you haven't prepared for at least once.

There are two kinds of walk-throughs, one that takes place in practice as I described, and another that takes place in a ballroom. When we go on the road, walk-throughs gets even more interesting. If we arrived two days before the game we would usually check into the hotel, go upstairs, put our stuff away then go out to get something to eat. Upon our return we would meet in a ballroom where the managers had taped an outline of the key and free throw lane.

I remember my first road trip to Chicago. We all met in this huge ballroom and I looked over and saw what looked like a box taped to the carpet, I leaned over and asked Darius Wright, a senior at the time, what the heck was going on. He never replied, but just had this look in his eye that told me I'd find out soon enough. At the team's retreat earlier that year I had remembered Flo Hartenstein mentioning something about walk-through being the worst, and that night I quickly found out why.

Coach Kent takes walk-throughs very seriously. In fact guys have not played if they didn't know what was going on in walk-though. The strange thing is that whenever someone messed up or looked out of sync during a walk-through, they usually ended up making the same mistakes in the game.

It was always a reward when Coach would say, "go ahead and go to bed; we will meet at breakfast in the morning," as opposed to the dreaded walk-through.

When there is a home game, there is no getting out of the off-the-court walk-through. The night before the game we have a pre-game team meal, usually at the Electric Station downtown. After dinner we meet at the Pittman Room at the Casanova Center. We watch a little film and then walk through the opponent's plays while incorporating our defensive plan. Our defensive plan usually changed depending on the opponent. Some teams play defense the same way every game, with what they call their system. But, we adjusted our defense on a regular basis to the way we wanted the opponent to play. If we had a team that shot the ball well, then we would take the ball out of the shooters' hands, not necessarily face-guarding, but more limiting the players' touches. Now this isn't uncommon for teams to do, after all our opponents tried to do it every game to at least one of our three best players. The difference for us was that we were not only good enough at it, but we could execute it against more than one player at a time.

It's foolish to think that you are going to be able to shut down every player on the floor every game. A lot of times there are players who are so good that they are going to get their points. Usually it is the other players that you have to be concerned about. This was one of the reasons we were so tough this year offensively. We had three big-time scorers in Luke, Luke, and Freddie, guys who could go for 30 points a night if they wanted to. It is all but impossible to shut down all three every game, not to mention that we had guys in other positions who were consistent in what they provided. Anthony Lever and James Davis provided a consistent three-point threat that put pressure on any team when the big three were out, not to mention the presence that Big Chris Christofferson had.

FEELING GOOD

Our first regular season game was against Alabama State. It was the first game of our home tournament. We got our scout tape a few days before and did the regular preparation. Before each game the coaches hand out a scouting report that is about five to six pages long. It consists of the team's plays and the tendencies of the players, along with keys to victory and a summary of the opponent's strengths and weaknesses. The coaches were not going to fool anybody by telling us that Alabama State was a good team. The plan was simple, play our game and focus on getting better.

The game was just like that; we played our style of game and got better. It was also a blowout, 92-52. We were able to get out and run, work on our defense against a quicker athletic driving team, and, most importantly, get some real game experience for every player. The format of the tournament was three games in three days. Coach Kent wanted to make sure and, not only play everyone, but also make sure he didn't wear any of the starters out.

The following game against Western Michigan was no different, another blowout, 91-48, and some more valuable experience for every player. After the game the coaches made sure that our goals were clear. We wanted to get better every game, regardless of the opponent. The third and final game against Long Beach State was no different than the first two games, another blowout, 97-67!

Overall the tournament was a success, 3-0 and we played better each game. Before our last game I sat down in the stands to watch the end of the Alabama State-Western Michigan game. Realizing that Alabama State was going to lose and go home 0-3, I thought about how quickly a season can turn for some teams. In reality they were probably finished at that point, all the hard work in the summer, all the talk of winning and getting to the NCAA tournament most likely finished with those three games. Their season was most likely already finished and they had just begun.

Meanwhile, our season was just beginning and we were feeling pretty good. After the Long Beach State game, talk immediately turned to our next opponent, Louisville. During the summer they ended a poorly handled departure of Hall of Fame coach Denny Crum by bringing in the highly regarded Rick Pitino. Before coach even told us, we knew they would be playing their first game on ESPN the next afternoon.

Their game was also a blowout from the start, throwing Pitino's patented pressing style at their opponent every time. The game was out of control within about 10 minutes, and in Pitino's first game at his new school, things were looking pretty good. I was surprised. I thought they would be improved, but wasn't sure if they had the athletes to implement Pitino's style of play that had been so successful at Kentucky. After the day off we were back at practice Monday with only five days until our first big game, Louisville at the Rose Garden in the Portland Jam. The Portland Jam is an annual game that was designed with the idea of giving the Portland fan base an opportunity to see us play without making the two-hour drive to Eugene. Each year it became more and more successful.

The first thing Coach said was to not be fooled by Louisville's game the day before. Reminding us that we were the better team and that we were going to give them a lesson in fast break basketball. Coach Kent always did a good job of keeping the team positive. I occasionally referred to him as the politician because he could sell you on anything. You could come away from a heart-breaking loss and the next day he would make it seem like the loss was not only a good thing, but that we needed it to get better. The funny thing was that it usually worked, with the exception of the beginning of the year and the Cal and Stanford games we never lost more than one game in a row, and usually went on streaks of four or five wins at a time.

The intensity in practice that week was at another level. We spent a great deal of time working on the full-court press Louisville would be frantically running against us. We worked on it so much that week that, by the time the game came around, we couldn't wait for them to try and press us. We saw the press as an opportunity to get into our favorite and most exciting part of the game, the fast break.

We chartered a bus and drove up to Portland the day before the game. We checked in to our hotel and then went to the annual banquet dinner at the Oregon Sports Hall of Fame in downtown Portland. After eating and socializing for a few minutes, we headed back to the hotel and immediately met in the ballroom for the walk-through. The walk-through was spent going through their plays and, most importantly, the press, which we knew they would be constantly throwing at us during the game. The walk-through went smoothly. We huddled up, gave a chant of "OREGON" and went to our rooms.

Game day is always long, especially if the game is later than 7 p.m. This one was. We usually get a chance to sleep in, and then meet for the team breakfast. After that we usually watch some film and then head over to the arena to shoot around. The shoot-around is more than just shooting around; this is the time where we walk through their plays again and run a few of our own plays, basically the fine-tuning. We are usually only there for about an hour.

At the end of the shoot-around we split up and line up at the free-throw line at each end. We shoot 20 free throws and the three guys who miss the least have a shoot-off. For such a simple little game there is a great deal of pride and bragging rights that go to the winner, and, like so many things in sports, nobody remembers who comes in second or third. In addition to lightening things up on game day, when some teams can be wound a little too tight, the competition helped us to become one of the best free throw shooting teams in the country.

After walk-through we head back to the hotel and get some rest. Some of the guys take naps; others just make sure they are off their feet. Usually about 3 p.m. we have a pre-game meal that includes chicken, pasta, salads, and lots of water and juice. After that we relax for about an hour and then get taped in Clay's room. The taping sessions are another part of the day that takes a long time. On the road only Clay comes so 10 guys have to get taped within about 45 minutes. Even though this is one of the longer parts of the day, it is usually the most relaxed. Most of the guys joke around and watch a game that's on television while we wait.

We always head over to the arena an hour-and-a-half before tip-off. This time is filled with getting some shots up and getting loose. Forty minutes before tip-off we meet back in the locker room, this is the chalk talk portion. Coach has usually written and drawn an array of keys and plays on the dry-erase board. For the Louisville game you could tell he was excited, and for good reason. He was matching up against one of the best coaches in college basketball.

Just like on Monday of that week, he again told us that this was not the Kentucky or even Louisville of old. "They have the same players as a year ago when we beat them by 26" he continued. We all expected a battle, and this would be our first big test of the year.

The game started a little sloppy. They were trying to press as hard as they could, and we were trying to transition as hard as we could. After a few minutes we settled down and began to slowly pull away. By halftime we had built a solid lead and appeared to be in control. At halftime a lot of the talk was about how they were going to try and jump on us in the second half, however, we also knew that they were tired. Without an exception to the rule every time we played a team that was supposed to be either well conditioned or a fast-breaking team, one thing happened. By halftime they were exhausted, and the majority of the time we knew it.

This game was no different. The talk for Louisville had been about how well conditioned they were and how their players had lost so much weight from their grueling conditioning. However, as we sat in the locker room, we couldn't wait to play the second half.

As the second half began they tried to get back into it, but every time they made a play we answered and kept the margin at 15-20 point the rest of the way. After the game we shook their hands and they looked completely worn out. After shaking hands the annual MVP award was handed out. Without much drama the award had gone to Freddie who had supplied an array of dunks and slashing moves on his way to 20 points, six rebounds.

In the locker room everyone was excited. I don't think we had realized how much we wanted to win the game. In the media room Rick Pitino was finishing up his interview when he had this to say, "Oregon is a terrific basketball team and certainly we had our hands full." At that point in the year and for our team and our program, his words seemed pretty gratifying. We indeed were not only getting better, but also starting to realize it as a team.

That night we got some dinner and went back to the hotel to get some rest, for tomorrow we were on our way to Massachusetts to face UMASS, the team we faced in the Portland Jam the previous year. This would be our first road game and would be an important step towards every team's goal of getting into the Top 25.

Rid easily getting into the paint.

CHAPTER 3
The Road

"If you can win at home, you're halfway to being a great team;
the other half is winning on the road"

Each year Coach Kent talks about the excitement of heading onto the road.
He's certainly not talking about the excitement of the long plane rides, bus rides,
or the hotels. The excitement Coach makes reference to is the unfriendly
environments that force teams to come together on and off the floor. At home,
especially at Mac Court, the crowd and the environment can make up for a slow
start, or a few bad plays, not to mention that the buzz at Mac Court always
provided extra energy. On the road however, is when you have to be the
sharpest. Those same slow starts and few bad plays can lose games. When
you're playing on the road the little mistakes are always the ones that cost you a
victory. Especially this year when we didn't lose a game by more than seven
points the entire regular season. Each game came down to executing down the
stretch.

At one point my first year Coach Kent had t-shirts made that said, "Oregon
Road Warriors,." We all thought maybe Oregon had a new NBA or CBA team
and he was wearing one of their promotional t-shirts. However, we soon
realized the importance of winning on the road. In 1999-2000, the majority of
our big wins came on the road. Without those wins we would have been
playing in the NIT instead of the NCAA tournament. Last year, we not only
lost at home, but all of our big losses came on the road. This time with those
losses we not only missed the NCAA, but the NIT too. So coming into this

season there was a strong emphasis on getting back to being a strong road team, and the UMASS game was our first opportunity.

Nobody was particularly excited for the flight from Portland to Massachusetts. It would include stops in Denver, Chicago, and finally Hartford, Conn., before a 45-minute bus ride to Springfield, Mass. The long flight wasn't the only concern. This was the first time a lot of the guys had flown since the 9/11 tragedy. Some of the players were afraid to fly before, and the events of that day only intensified those fears.

We woke up about 8:30 Sunday morning, a day after the Louisville game, and, within a few hours, we were on our way. We arrived at the hotel that night at a little after midnight. Although the game against UMASS wasn't until Tuesday, rest was the top priority that night so we went straight to bed.

The road is filled with one meeting after another. After a few road trips I began to realize that there was a method to the madness. In an effort to make sure that guys stayed focused and got enough rest, each meeting, practice or team activity was designed around breaking the day up into time periods that eliminated any long amounts of free time. Although players regularly complained, the method was surprisingly effective. A few road trips into the season we had become pretty well programmed. I actually felt out of sync if we were given any lengthy amount of free time. By the end of the season the program was what kept us focused.

The coaches rarely change the day before a game routine. It includes a team breakfast, a light practice, a study session, dinner, and an evening activity, usually a movie with the team. Because we were not only playing but also staying in the birthplace of basketball, Springfield, our activity that day included a trip to the Basketball Hall of Fame. Only a handful of guys had actually been there so it was a new experience for nearly everybody.

The Hall of Fame was different than anybody expected, sort of like seeing the White House for the first time and realizing that it's a lot smaller than it looks on TV and the movies. The Hall of Fame was not only run down, but was really in its last stages. The next year employees would be moving all the displays into a state of the art facility across the parking lot. Still in construction, the new building was beginning to look like what we thought the Hall of Fame would be.

With the exception of our disappointment at its appearance, the Hall of Fame was still pretty amazing from a basketball player's and fan's perspective. Along with a great deal of history, it had a lot of character. Before we left we took a picture on a giant staircase that ran right in front of the basket and section of floor that Michael Jordan had hit his game-winning shot in the finals against Utah on.

Of course this only brought anti-Utah comments directed at Mark and I from the rest of the team, after all we both grew up in Salt Lake. Secretly I still believed that Utah deserved to win the championship that year, but knew that any such comment would only generate more Jazz-bashing. However, I briefly contemplated setting a match to the floor and running out of there, restoring the pride of Bryan Russell who was left on the floor when Jordan drained his historic shot. Fortunately better judgment won over and we left for dinner.

That night we watched the Texas-Colorado Big XII football game while we ate in Chili's. We cheered for the defeat of Texas with the hope of that it would give our football team a shot at the Rose Bowl. After dinner we went back and finished the evening off with a walk-through.

The next morning, we felt not only prepared, but excited for our next test. Similar to Louisville, Umass had basically the same team from the previous season's game, which we had won. We felt confident that this game would be no different.

Before the game every team huddles up right before the players go onto the floor and yells some kind of team chant. Each year the chant changes. The idea behind the chant is to not only to get everybody pumped up, but also there seems to be something reassuring about repetition before a game.

Every team yells something different. Back in the day when the Bulls won all their championships, they would yell the same thing before every game. One guy would say, "What time is it?" followed by the rest of the team yelling, "Game time."

My first year, Alex Scales would yell, "Are ya with me?" Then the rest of the team would reply, "Oh yeah, We hold the fort. We ain't going no where!"

Some chants are corny, filled with slang and a little over the top; others are simple. However, each year the previous chant is replaced with something supposedly new and creative.

This year we couldn't decide on a chant until a few games into the season, and, of course, any time you put a basketball team in a circle and try and get them to harmonize, it can be an embarrassing and a laughing matter. We had finally settled on, "We right here, we ain't going any where," with a little pause in the middle. We then finished with, "We right here, bring your team cause we don't care!" This seemed to work until the trip to Umass, before the game we did our regular chant, went out on to the floor and warmed up. With about 12 minutes before tip-off, the teams headed into the locker rooms for their final chalk talk.

In each arena the locker rooms are set up so the two teams enter the floor from different directions. However, in this particular arena, the two locker rooms were just down the hall from each other. When we were coming out the locker room door, the UMASS team was in the middle of its huddle, getting ready to start its chant.

Not one of us could believe our ears. What we heard was a faster-paced version of our exact pre-game chant. When we first came onto the floor 30 minutes before the game, we were on the other side of the arena so we knew that the Umass players couldn't have heard our chant and sarcastically repeated it.

We usually do an abbreviated version before we head onto the floor for the last time. However, after what had just taken place, we gave a simple "DUCKS!!" chant and headed onto the floor, not only confused at the fact that UMass had the same exact chant but that we had heard them say it. Without having to say anything we all knew the chant would be changed for the following game.

The game was a back-and-forth battle. We seemed to jump on them from the start, but they fought back into the game through our bad shots and poor execution. By the time the end of the game had rolled around, we were down three with only seconds remaining. After the last game, I think we thought we were going to fly cross-country and beat them by 25, just like we had beaten everyone else up to that point. However, by halftime we knew we were in for a fight, and that it could easily come down to the final minutes.

Rid dribbled to halfcourt and we called a timeout to set up a play for a three-pointer that would tie the game. Anthony and James checked in to join Jackson, Freddie and Rid, giving us five guys who could all shoot the three-pointer.

We decided to spread them out and run a motion set called weave. Weave is where you basically line up around the three-point line and the player with the ball dribbles at another player, not only handing the ball off, but screening the defender at the same time.

This seemed like a good strategy that would create a mismatch with the bigger forwards having to guard smaller quicker players. After a few hand-offs Jackson got the ball, dribbled along the three-point line, jumped into the air trying to draw a defender. But he ended up getting stuck in the air and throwing the pass right into the hands of a Umass player.

I don't think anybody was more disappointed than Luke Jackson. The look on his face was evidence enough. After a foul and some free throws, the game was over. Every player was stunned; we really couldn't believe that we had lost. Umass had played a great game and was able to get its crowd into it, but, in the back of our minds, we kept thinking we were going to win even when we got down. I don't think we were overconfident as much as we felt sure that if we played hard we would win.

Jackson had taken the loss hard, and throughout the course of the night apologized for the errant pass. No one on the team held him responsible, but as he mentioned that night he had put so much into his spring and summer to be in that position and come through with the big play. Some guys might let something like that get into their head, but he went back to work in practice, playing harder than anybody else the next week.

We headed back to Eugene disappointed, but feeling like we learned a lesson about playing on the road, again growing unnoticeably. We had jumped on them early and had failed to finish them off. One of the worst things you can do is let a team get back into a game they should lose by 20. Unfortunately that's easier said than done.

THE WEEK BEFORE PORTLAND

Our next game was not only another road game, but a game in which we felt we could get some of the kinks worked out of our system. Portland was a struggling team that was completely overmatched. Each year we talk about how, for the smaller schools in the state, this is their biggest game of the year, and how they play better every time. The attitude in practice that week was we were going to go up there and put a whupping on them, everyone would play, and the game would be over by halftime.

We had an intense week of practice, filled with watching game tape of the sickening loss to Umass. We had thought we had played hard, but as they say, "the eye in the sky never lies," and this time that was true. As we watched the tape, it seemed like we were watching someone else. The reasons we lost were more than just failing to finish the team off when we had the chance. We didn't play hard, and we didn't play together! Playing together was something that was a point of emphasis in practice that week.

We bused to Portland Saturday and prepared to play the following day. We drove straight to the gym and had a quick shoot-around.

The game was at 3 p.m. the next day so we weren't going to get a chance to shoot around the next day. Things went well; the mood was light and we again felt that we were ready.

The crowd arrived, mostly wearing Oregon green and gold, more of an advantage for us than for the home team Pilots.

The game got off to a sluggish start. The Pilots didn't seem to fear us, and we actually seemed a little surprised by that. We had gotten down, but worked our way back into the game and a lead. Halftime in the locker room was not a pleasant place. We were all embarrassed, and determined to play more inspired in the second half.

Coach Kent entered the locker room a few minutes after we did. Immediately the room went silent, "You're playing just hard enough to get beat" he said.

The problem was we could locate the itch, but we seemed to be unsure about scratching it. We knew we weren't doing the things it took to win. A four-game win streak, filled with success at every turn seemed longer than a game and a half ago; it felt like last season.

We ran out of the locker room determined to play better. The second half was however, not going to be a blowout. Freddie had picked up some early fouls, and spent the majority of the game on the bench, fouling out early in the second half. The game went back and forth somehow they seemed to hang around. We had again failed to put the game away when we had the chance, and they were now playing with a great deal of confidence. With about a minute left we were up by three. I went into the game to provide some foul shooting and within five seconds went to the line. I went through my regular routine and put up the first foul shot. It circled around, going half in and then spun out. I didn't panic, but afterwards thought Coach Kent probably didn't think I would have to shoot the potentially game-deciding foul shots.

After some negative reinforcement from the crowd, I gathered myself and put the other free throw in without fooling with the rim. Portland passed the ball in and raced down the floor. With his team down by four, the Pilots' point guard penetrated and dished to my man in the corner. Immediately I knew his shot was going in. I had foolishly tried to stop the penetration and the threat of two points, and in the process had given up a three-pointer.

We were still up one with time for their comeback running out, so I didn't panic. We took the ball out against their full court pressure and I somehow received the pass again, this time at half court. I was fouled quickly, and at this point could only imagine Coach Kent's thought process. After he had put me in, I had missed a free throw and had given up a three-pointer, and was going to the line to shoot two more with the Ducks up only one.

I, of course, didn't think about that at the line, and somehow slid in the first shot. After taking a deep breath, I calmly put the second one up and in.

The free throws had put us up by three and we were seconds away from a close victory on the road.

After the trip to the line Portland called a timeout to set up their next move. Meanwhile, our huddle was filled with frustration at the situation, but we were clear that whatever happened, we would not to give up a three-pointer. In order to do this, Coach kept emphasizing, "Switch everything!!!"

Similar to their last play the Pilots quickly dribbled up the floor, and ran a ball screen. Rid and Jackson were guarding the ball and the screener. When their best shooter came off the screen, there was some confusion on who should guard whom. By the time the two Ducks had figured it out an uncontested three-pointer was on its way. After the ball had sizzled through the net the game was tied with seconds left. We took a timeout and set up a drive-and-kick play with the ball in Rid's hands.

Freddie had already fouled out and we were forced to try and run a play in a matter of seconds. After the play was selected, the focus switched to making sure that we got the last shot. The game was tied and the worst-case scenario was going to overtime.

Rid received the ball and drove up the left sideline. Another defender left Anthony on the far side and went to double-team the ball. Rid, recognizing this, looked to pass the ball across the court with the hopes of still getting off a game-winning shot. As soon as the ball left his hands, you could tell it wasn't going to get there. The weak side defender, Corky Rochin, went into the passing lane and, in slow motion, intercepted the pass intended for Anthony. Anthony had been going for the ball too, and, in an attempt get a hand on it, unintentionally collided with Rochin. A whistle blew. The ref signaled to the scorer's table that the foul was on, "Black No. 34." Everyone's heart sank to the floor. What had seemed like a close game heading to overtime now had become a potential loss resting on two foul shots.

Rochin was not a great foul shooter and didn't seem comfortable at the line. With time still on the clock, even if he made both free throws, we would still have a chance to get a last second shot off.

His first free throw was hard off the backboard and brought us hope. Rochin appeared to gather his thoughts and put up the next shot effortlessly. It went in and we were down one, scrambling to decide what play to run. We took another time-out and decided to get the ball inbound as close to half court as possible, getting the best shot we could. With so little time, it's not like you can set up any real strategically oriented play. A lot of those situations is getting a good look and hoping that one shot can erase a disappointing game.

James got the ball and raced down the right sideline, getting about 10 feet behind the three-point line and throwing up a shot that had a chance. It banked off the backboard, circled the rim and fell into a Portland player's hands as the horn sounded. The game was over, not only had we been upset, but embarrassed. In the space of a week we had gone from undefeated and feeling pretty good to one game over .500 and uncertain about the state of not just our team, but our season.

The locker room was quiet. There were a few tears, but mostly shocked looks. This time Luke Ridnour felt responsible for the loss because of his turnover at the end. The only bright spot from the game was the inspired play of Luke Jackson, who scored 28 points on 9-of-18 shooting.

Coach Kent didn't have a lot to say. He was as shocked as anybody. He had realized that Portland would play its best basketball, but had no idea that we would play our worst.

When the coaches had finished speaking to us, they left the room and it was just the team. No one said a word. Nobody knew what to say. You could see the same look on each person's face. We had officially hit rock bottom!!!

When we arrived back in Eugene, we had a meeting as soon as we got off the bus. Every person sat in a chair trying to figure out what had happened to our team. Nobody had the answers. The coaches asked if anybody had any ideas. A few guys replied, but the answers didn't feel like the real solution to what was happening to our team. After the meeting it didn't feel like we had accomplished much, but oftentimes when you lose it doesn't feel like anything helps. With another crucial road game coming up, once again we were going to have to get back to the basics.

MINNESOTA

As it was the week after the UMASS loss, practice was again spirited. After hitting rock bottom we felt there was no place to go but up! As a team we desperately needed a win the following week. Our next opponent was Minnesota; a team that had struggled early and also faced a must-win situation. On film they looked ripe for the picking, and we left with our confidence back in place and ready to erase the now popular "poor road team" tag that the media had placed on us.

Whenever we travel, we travel in coat and tie. Not only do we get a lot of positive comments, but I always felt that it seemed to help us treat the trip like business instead of a vacation. Although not everybody liked the idea of wearing the suit and tie, whenever we saw another team that was in sweats or jeans in an airport, we all quietly felt a little better about the way we were dressed. The real downside to dressing in a suit and tie is that you are in it the entire day, which is usually spent in undersized plane seats and uncomfortable bus rides. However, coming from a year at a junior college where we had a 22-hour bus ride one way, I occasionally reminded myself that it could be a lot worse.

We left early with the idea of getting to Minnesota a few days early to get acclimated. When we finally arrived, we were immediately surprised by the cold weather. Jay Anderson, who is from Minnesota, had tried to describe the cold, but the first time we walked outside, it felt like someone poking our faces with needles. I had grown up in Utah and was used to the cold and snow, but this was unlike anything I had ever felt.

We had arrived too late to get a walk through in, so we were told to read our scouting reports and meet for breakfast in the morning. The schedule would be the same as other trips, but this time we would have a chance to visit the Mall of America, supposedly one of the world's biggest malls. After a normal practice we came back to the hotel, showered and we were off to the Mall.

The Mall of America is quite surreal. Imagine four of the biggest malls you have ever been in, and multiple that by eight, then throw four levels of the same thing on the top of each other. Then add the amusement park that sits in the middle of the mall. Not many of us had seen anything like this, and after only seeing about 10 percent of what the mall had to offer; we never wanted to see anything like it again. It was one of those situations that was more frustrating than fun. There was so much to see, but you would have to come every day for a week to see the entire mall.

We ate dinner, went to a movie, and went back to the hotel for a walk-through. The mall, dinner, and the movie took about four hours. So, with plenty of time to spare, we had our walk-through and went to bed feeling rested and excited for an important game that could get us back on track.

Game day was as usual, Minnesota was a great environment to play basketball, and we were all awaiting tip-off. The game was to be televised on ESPN, which we thought would provide a chance for the rest of the country to see us play. In the local papers, all the talk was about how Minnesota was at a crossroad; they had just come off a disappointing loss, and had been underachieving thus far. The paper also mentioned a heart-to-heart team meeting that seemed not only ironic but eerily similar to our meeting that same week. We knew we would have to play our best basketball to date to win the game, and certainly welcomed the challenge.

The game started out like feeling like we had gotten back the key that was missing. However, Minnesota's players looked like they had found their game as well. The entire game was a battle; each team answered the other on the defensive and offensive ends. As time began to run out in the second half, so too had our hopes of winning the game. After battling the entire game we failed to make plays down the stretch. Their crowd had come alive and one would have to wonder if we had played the game in "The PIT" what would have happened. I have felt like we had won a number of games at home because of the our crowd, but never had I felt so sure that the difference in the game was simply playing in the opponent's arena. Sure, we didn't do everything perfect, but we played hard, made some good plays, and, in the final minutes, still had a chance to win.

When the buzzer finally sounded, we had a bittersweet feeling. We had played not just harder, but had played some pretty good basketball. Yet it also felt like we were right back where we had started. Minnesota, on the other hand, appeared to have hit on all cylinders and looked like a team coming into its own. The locker room was again quiet. Coach Kent hardly ever lost his temper after games, and wasn't about to do so now. There was a lot more basketball to play. Again we were all disappointed. We had fought so hard and it felt like we were doing all we could.

In his usual tone, coach talked about things like learning something from the game, and using this as a growing experience. He closed by saying that we weren't there yet, and if we wanted to reach our goals we would have to get back to work that week. After a locker room visit by former Oregon great Terrell Brandon, we loaded onto the bus and headed back to the hotel. We arrived in Eugene the next afternoon. There was no time for a day off; our next opponent was Pepperdine, a team that had beaten UCLA, USC, and BYU. We knew they would be traveling to Eugene with not only their confidence, but also a swagger in their step, looking to upset another big team.

Only two weeks had passed since the media had posed questions about the possibility of the our team peaking too early after four decisive wins. Our return was met with even more questions, this time about our ability to win on the road, something that would be crucial not just to winning a PAC-10 championship, but getting to the NCAA tournament.

THE START OF A STREAK

With only two games until the start of the conference season it was crucial that we gain some form of momentum. At 4-3, we were ourselves at a crossroads. A losing pre-season would probably assure us of a trip to the NIT. The coaches and the players felt it was important to not only get our confidence back, but that we set some goals as a team.

At the start of the year we had talked about winning the PAC-10 championship, going to the NCAA tournament and going undefeated at home. Along the way we had sort of forgotten that in between you have to play a lot of games. So the few days we had between the Minnesota trip and the Pepperdine game were spent focusing on setting and reaching team goals. Our first goal was to go 5-0 at home before we headed to Arizona for the second half of that series.

When you head into the conference season, it is important that you are playing good basketball. Since I have been here no team has had a terrible pre-season and then waltzed into the conference and dominated. With two important home games and then a four-game set with the Arizona schools, we knew in the back of our mind that we could easily come out of the first two weeks of the conference 0-4 and 4-7, and a long way from post-season play.

However, we had finally started to do what this team always did, play the games and let other people talk about the consequences. In order to add a spark to practice that week, Coach decided to scrimmage. We usually scrimmaged early in the year to break up weeks of practice while waiting for our first game. When Coach announced this week's scrimmage, we immediately got excited.

The scrimmage always did two things — it stirred things up in terms of practice schedule, and it gave the guys who weren't getting a lot of time a chance to shine. I always looked forward to scrimmages, and was excited for this one after not getting onto the floor the previous game. If nothing else, I thought it would be a chance to get up and down the floor and have some fun.

The scrimmage always consists of different line-ups, again following the theme of mixing things up. I was put with Freddie and Anthony at the guard spot. By the time the scrimmage was done, I had somehow taken 11 shots and made 10 of them, six being three-pointers. I thought if anything it would get me a few minutes in the next game. However, the next day in practice I was with the green team, which is the first team, and Freddie had been moved to the White team. I wasn't the only one who was surprised. I honestly didn't think much of it; Coach had mixed lineups in practice before and this seemed like the same drill. When the end of practice came around and we got ready for walk-through, Freddie told me to stay on the floor. Confused, I said, "that's O.K., you go ahead."

That night I got a call from Coach Kent, "I don't know if you are going to start tomorrow but, if you do, I suggest you make it hard to get the spot back."

I hadn't thought anything of the lineup switch since leaving Mac Court, and, after talking to Coach Kent really thought that a guy like James, who had a great 20-point game against Minnesota, probably deserved it more. I went to bed that night assuming that it was a simple ploy to try and get Freddie to play harder after a string of poor games.

I began to have flashbacks of my first year. After an early season loss, the coaches were again frustrated with Freddie's effort. For some strange reason they threw me into the starting lineup for the rest of the pre-season until the conference opener against Oregon State when they decided Freddie had realized he needed to work harder. His response had been a brilliant game that started off with three three-pointers to put our opponent out of the game early. It seemed to work a few years ago and perhaps they thought it might do the same again.

The next day at the shoot-around I was a little uncomfortable. The competitor in me wanted to start and play every minute, but the other side wondered whether I had really earned it, or if it was just another ploy to get Freddie to play hard. If that was the case, why was I the bait?

It turned out I would be starting that night, and I honestly thought it would be a one-night deal. Freddie would learn his lesson, and things would be back to normal.

I came out with a lot of energy, knowing that if I worked hard the results couldn't be bad. I didn't make any great offensive plays, In fact I think I only scored one basket off seven shots, but there was one play that stood out. There was a long rebound that was heading out of bounds on the opposite side of the team bench. I decided to go after it, diving over the front row of seats while flipping the ball blindly behind me to Luke Jackson. I was stuck behind the row of seats and, at that point, assumed that the other team had caught my desperation pass and was on their way to the other end. I ran behind the courtside folding chairs and finally just jumped over them back onto the court.

To my surprise we still had possession of the ball and I found myself wide open. I caught the ball and realized that if I could hit the shot the place would go nuts. Mac Court is the kind of place where hustle and hard work and defense are rewarded just as much, if not more, than spectacular dunks and fancy passing.

When I got the pass I had no intention of doing anything else but shooting it. So in stride I put it up and realized it was going to be a little short. My excuse, of course, was that I was tired from the previous play.

There is a not too old saying, shooters should be the best rebounders, after all they can usually tell where it's going as soon as it leaves their hand. Well, I was an average shooter, and certainly not a rebounder, but I knew this shot was short. I raced after the ball as soon as it left my hand, bobbled it a few times, finally caught it in stride and dribbled under the basket to the other side of the floor before finally passing the ball out top to settle things down.

This was met with a roar from the crowd and, with the exception of senior night and a pair of last second, game-winning passes against Arizona State my first year, this was one of my proudest moments in the confines of Mac Court.

By the end of the first half the game was a blowout, and Freddie was back to his old self, scoring points and playing harder than he had all year. At halftime we were up again and somehow that same great feeling from the beginning of the year was back in the locker room.

Was it because I was inserted into the starting lineup? Probably not, but it felt like something had changed. This time the locker room was filled with smiles, and it felt good to be home after a three-game losing streak on the road. The second half was no different than the first. Everyone played, and played well.

After the game things felt normal; the excitement was back. Coach Kent strolled in and looked like he had been holding his breath for three games and could finally breathe again. He mentioned how Freddie had stepped up and how that's what we needed if we were going to win the PAC-10. He finished by saying we had one more game to get ready for the Arizona schools, so "let's make sure we continue to get better."

After we teamed it up to a cheer of "family," Coach pulled me aside and said, "I hope you know your role." I, of course, gave the "I know what you're talking about" look until he actually told me what he really meant, "You are our energy guy."

He went on to make references to how the crowd will respond to playing hard and how Oregon fans are some of the most intelligent fans in the country. "Some of them have been coming to games for 30 years, still sitting in the same seats," he said in a fatherly tone.

Coach Kent always talked passionately about the Mac Court fans, regularly reflecting on the days when he and Coach Graham roamed the same gym known as the "Kamikaze Kids." I often felt that he enjoyed the noise and cheers of the crowd as much now as he did back in the 1970's.

The next game I was informed that I would be starting again, and was a little surprised, Freddie had a great game and it felt like things had finally gotten back to normal. Northern Arizona would be our final tune-up before our first conference game against Arizona State. This game was no different than the previous one. The crowd was finally starting to really get into the games and it felt like we were back into midseason form. The game was never close and featured and array of dunks from Freddie and no-look passes for easy baskets from Rid. And, our defense actually started to take shape.

From our first exhibition game until this game the talk in the first timeout always included Litz informing us of how many consecutive stops we had gotten on the defensive end. Litz wanted to make this a point of emphasis this year. He felt it was important to not just get consecutive stops, but that by doing so we could measure the success of our defense by more than just points and field goal percentage.

If a team could consistently put together defensive stops, it not only influenced the score, but also helped a team like ours get into transition and run the fast break. Defensively, one of the worst things you can do as a team is trade baskets. It doesn't make a lot of sense to score at one end and then let the other team go down and also score. Litz wanted us to get to the point where we were getting five stops in a row. Often times, including the game against Pepperdine, we got not just five but ten.

After putting two well-played games together for the first time in three weeks, we started to get back some of the confidence that we had lost over those same three weeks. Coach Kent throughout the year always made references to the next game being the biggest one of the year. Although it sounded like a cliché, it was seldom untrue, regardless of how good the opponent was. We had four days until Arizona State, and once again this was be the biggest game of the year to that point.

Freddie dunking as usual…with authority!

CHAPTER 4
Already Here

"There is one quality which one must posses to win, and that is definiteness of purpose, the knowledge of what one wants, and the burning desire to possess it." — Napoleon Hill

For the first time in years conference games would be played in December. In the past the first conference games were in January. However, because of the resurrection of the PAC-10 tournament, the games would have to be played earlier than ever.

In the PAC-10, games are regularly played on Thursday and Saturday to eliminate travel problems. Each team has a travel partner that is located in the same geographical area. For example our travel partner is Oregon State. Whoever we play on Thursday the Beavers play on Saturday, and vice versa.

This year everything was done differently. Usually teams play all the teams in the conference once, either at home or on the road. Then, after the first nine games, teams play one another one more time at the opposite place they played the first time. Not only does this spread the games around, but it also makes it so those two teams don't play each other on consecutive weekends. However, because of the first PAC-10 tournament in a decade, schedules would be anything but normal this year. We would be playing host to the Arizona schools, and then after a non-conference home game, would head down to Arizona and play the Wildcats and Sun Devils again. Other wacky schedules included UCLA and USC heading to the Washington schools on different weekends. The best of all featured Stanford hosting Cal on a Thursday and traveling an hour to play them two days later on Saturday in Berkeley.

With a lackluster pre-season that had its up and downs, we were anything but the favorite for the PAC-10 title. Every major pre-season publication had us picked to finish in the lower half of the conference, and to that point we looked to be on schedule to do so.

We all knew that we had played some poor basketball and probably lost two games we should have won. But, in our locker room it was not about a disappointing pre-season, but instead about winning one game, a Thursday match-up with Arizona State. Any time you play Arizona after Arizona State, it's difficult not to look past the Sun Devils to the consistently ranked Arizona. However, our goal from the start of practice was to take it one game at a time.

Last season we suffered an embarrassing home loss by about 25 points, which happened to come on the heels of an impressive win against Arizona two days before. We not only had a little revenge on our minds, but we also wanted to prove to the conference that we would be the team to beat. We didn't walk around saying "We're the team to beat;" it was not that kind of thing. Our team was never a cocky, or an arrogant team. We just always had a quiet calm; every guy on the team believed in the guy next to him.

That week in practice we were especially focused. Finals had been finished for over a week, and every day in practice it was about beating Arizona State. It's not hard to describe a team that's focused, but our team was different. The way we were focused was always different. There would be times that we all knew we were ready to play, but the mood would be extremely loose, including joking right up until we got to the arena. Other times our mood would be quiet, and felt like we might be a little tight, which usually meant a quiet bus ride to the arena.

At this point in the season we were still finding ways to be successful. We had struggled, and knew that we would need to play better. Over the months we had been slowly changing. We knew we had a great deal of potential as a team, but we didn't know how to tap into it consistently. There were times the preseason seemed like a hit-and-miss situation.

With the exception of the postseason, conference games are the most exciting. The level of excitement for every game doubles. A game against the worst team in the league can easily turn into an upset or a blowout. Along with the excitement, there is a change in the level of play. Things get a lot more physical, and the defense becomes more intense. With the addition of the PAC-10 tournament every game would be played with something on the line because only the top eight teams would make it to the tournament in LA. Oftentimes the schools that were out of the running for either a conference title or a postseason bid would be playing to finish the season instead of playing to win. This year would be different. The talk throughout the year was about each school having a legitimate shot at the tournament and an automatic bid to the NCAA tournament. I wondered throughout the year if the last place teams that hadn't won three games in a row since the first of the year against sub-par competition really thought they could win three in a row against the best teams in the conference in LA. The focus of some teams was just to make it to the conference tournament. Ours was to make it as the No. 1 seed.

BEFORE THE GAME

The only bad thing about playing in Mac Court is that in December a lot of the students have gone home for their winter break. In years past we were usually playing a doormat team tuning up for the conference season. This year we played four conference games before school even started. We had no idea how loud the game would get. We had been telling the new guys about games in the past, and how the level of competition not only increases, but the energy of the crowd does too. It's funny, but for players the crowd is one of the most exciting parts of the game. Before every game there is always a conversation regarding the potential crowd noise, and a little exaggeration from the veteran players about wild games from seasons past. I think I have told the USC story 50 times.

In 1999, we were playing USC at home and the game came down to the final minutes. The Trojans' Brandon Granville had a pair of free throws to tie the game. Sensing the urgency the crowd stood and started to stomp on the wooden bleachers. Mac Court is not a young building by any means. One stomp on a far end can be felt in the third balcony. When the crowd started jumping up and down, the effect could be felt in more than one place. Intently watching Granville from the bench on the far end, I noticed that the entire basketball hoop was shifting side to side.

Doing a double take, I leaned over to former player David Jackson, "Dave is the hoop moving or am I?" I yelled over the noise of the crowd.

"The hoop is doing more than moving" he replied. By that time everyone had noticed the motion. This only encouraged the crowd even more.

The photographers and ball boys around the basket quickly moved a little farther away from the hoop than normal, apparently fearing a collapse.

Meanwhile USC head coach Henry Bibby was outraged, and tried to plead his case to the nearest official. Granville stood at the free throw line wondering if he should shoot or tell the ref that the hoop was moving. By this time the hoop was shifting by about six inches a side. The hoop was the last thing the refs were watching.

Finally realizing that he was going to have to shoot the ball, Granville put up a shot that on any other hoop would have going through without a trace of the rim.

However, this was not any other hoop or gym; this was Mac Court, home of the unexpected and unbelievable. Granville's free throw never had a chance and was sent off the rim as though it had been thrown from half court. By this point the refs had been persuaded to look at the hoop by Bibby, and the fact Granville had missed the free throw only excited the crowd even more.

The ref hustled over to the scorer's table and informed the people there that the first free throw would be shot over because the crowd was shaking the hoop.

This was probably one of the loudest moments I ever witnessed in Mac Court. The crowd was enraged, and couldn't believe it when the announcer came across the P.A. informed them of the ruling. About five minutes of constant unbearable noise from the crowd followed. They were determined not to stop, and didn't until Coach Kent grabbed the microphone at half court.

"We appreciate the noise, but please stop stomping" he said. The announcer then added that any more shaking would result in a technical foul. The people in the crowd weren't allowed to stomp, but they were just as loud.

In all the sporting events I had experienced — from professional to college and high school — I had never seen anything like that. In any other gym, we probably would have lost that game. I don't think I have ever seen or heard of a building affecting the outcome of a game in the way that Mac Court can. For years Mac Court has turned average teams into unbeatable, sometimes for an entire game. The greatest thing about this story is that each time it's retold, it gets better.

ASU

Although the game was being played over the break, Mac Court was all but full, and the fans had begun to make the transition between football and basketball. Before every home game we have a shoot-around and a pre-game meal. We usually have an hour or two between the meal and the 5:30 required arrival time. However, this being our first conference game of the year, everyone was there a little early, anxious to get some shots up, and even more focused. There was one smell that let you know it was game day, the smell of popcorn. When we come to the games we enter from the back door, which is a 10-foot distance from the locker room doors. As soon as you come through the doors, the only thing you smell is freshly made popcorn. I am the kind of guy who can go to the movie theater having just eaten a full meal and, as soon as I smell the popcorn, I am mysteriously hungry. I secretly wanted to eat a bag of it before every game, and I think Coach Kent actually did.

When we came through the doors the smell was there and it immediately felt like game day. We followed the normal pre-game routine and found ourselves in the team room 45 minutes before tip-off. Coach Kent had put together a highlight video. He turned off the lights and played it just about as loud as it could go. The video featured amazing dunks, long three-pointers, and, of course, some fancy passing. If anybody in the room was not ready to play, that video took care of it. After a few minutes of covering the game plan we met in the hall just outside the locker room.

We had finally come up with our new pre-game chant, and although it seemed a little silly, we used it anyway. We had decided to use a rap lyric from Puff Daddy's six-month old song that had been a bit altered. The original was as follows, "We ain't going nowhere, we ain't going nowhere; we can't be stopped now, cause it's bad boy for life." Bad boy is the self-created music label that Puff Daddy owned. A few of the guys on the team decided to put a little spin on the rap. "We ain't going nowhere, What? ... We ain't going nowhere; we can't be stopped now, cause its U O for life." I am not sure how many of the guys felt comfortable yelling that in a circle moving back and forth, but by the end of the year it had become part of who we were. In fact, I think as corny as the chant was we actually believed in what we were saying — every player would have a part of the University of Oregon for life.

THE GAME

Tip-off had finally arrived. We jumped on the Sun Devils from the start. In warm-ups they didn't look ready to play, and we had noticed and capitalized on that. The first half wasn't even close; it felt like we could run any play we wanted. Heading into the locker room we weren't necessarily surprised by the score, but more by how easy it had been. We had come into the game expecting a battle, and they had given up in the first half. The talk in the locker room had nothing to do with what they were doing as much as it was about staying focused and continuing to play hard.

The second half started the same way the first half had gone. We scored with ease, and our starters were resting on the bench, with the idea of resting for the game against 10th-ranked Arizona on Saturday. We were cruising along with about 10 minutes left and the game started to change. Arizona State started scoring and we had stopped because of poor shots and turnovers. Their starters were also on the bench, and their reserves had started to turn an absolute blowout into a 15-point game. The only problem for them was that they were running out of time. After a steal and a dunk before the buzzer, the game was over and we had won, 103-90. After having them down, we had failed to bury them.

After the game Coach Kent was excited for the victory, but his first concern was how we had finished the game. With a rematch in less than two weeks, the Sun Devils had exposed a weakness they had failed to realize the entire game. The way they had gotten back into the game was through penetrating off the drive, which resulted in either a foul or a lay-up. Up until that point they had been trying to uncharacteristically shoot the outside shot with the hopes of keeping up with us. This turned into easy baskets through the fast break, and a lopsided score. We knew that we had slipped in the last 10 minutes, but we also knew that we had played some great basketball.

After discussing the weaknesses in the game, we quickly switched our focus to Arizona. We knew that the Wildcats had beaten Oregon State after struggling early. We felt confident that they would come into the game and, just like every year, overlook us. We also felt confident that our team was turning the corner on an ugly preseason that felt like a constant learning process. We had learned something with each game, and, as a team, we were ready to start applying our knowledge.

ARIZONA

Since Coach Kent's been at Oregon, the team has stayed in a hotel the night before the Saturday conference game. A lot of teams around the country do something similar, the idea is to keep the players from staying out late and also losing focus. We had been expecting the announcement that we would be checking into the hotel Friday night, but it never came. I don't know if it was because Coach thought we were more focused than years past, but I know a lot of the guys wanted to sleep in their own beds the night before a big game. Whatever it was, we knew that with a bad performance we would be in a hotel the next home conference game.

Before the game both teams were on the floor stretching and shooting. We had been going through some structured shooting drills on our end of the floor. On the Arizona end, the Wildcat players were shooting NBA three-pointers and jokingly going one-on-one. It felt almost a little disrespectful, we were expecting a hard-fought game, and it looked like they were warming up for an all-star game.

In the locker room the talk was about how they weren't ready to play. At the time I didn't know if that was true. After all, they were probably one of the loosest teams in the conference, and had experienced a lot of success. When the game started it was obvious that we were going to have a good team game. Everyone looked like he was on top of his game. Luke Jackson was scoring from all over the court; Freddie was spectacular and efficient. Rid was making all the plays on offense and defense. James was draining threes from all the right spots at all the right times.

The biggest plays didn't come on the offensive end though. The defense changed the game. Luke Jackson had the assignment of guarding Arizona's do-everything Luke Walton, son of NBA great Bill Walton. Walton was kind of like a point guard who played small forward. He passed the ball better than most point guards around the country and the Wildcat offense relied heavily on his playmaking.

The other defensive key was Freddie's full court defense and half court ball pressure on Jason Gardner, who had opted to stay in school after initially declaring for the NBA draft. Similar to Walton he was crucial to the majority of what Arizona did on offense.

We headed to the locker room at the half with a 10-point lead, and a great deal of confidence. Coach Kent was excited, and came in a few minutes after we did, "(Lute Olson) is probably down there telling them that we aren't going to shoot that well in the second half," he said, "But he doesn't know how good of a shooting team we are, because we are going to shoot even better." As everyone shook his head in agreeing, we talked about cleaning up a few of the little things that had cost us an even bigger lead. "If we clean up these things, we'll beat em' by 25" Coach said as we teamed it up.

Coach Kent was wrong; we cleaned up the little things, but we didn't beat them by 25. We beat them by 30!

Other than that he seemed almost prophetic at halftime regarding our shooting. We had indeed gone on to shoot even better. Anytime they tried to make a run; we either answered with a big stop, or a huge three. The second half featured a lot of smiles, but didn't include any showboating or trash talking. We knew we had to face them in two weeks, and were content with

scoring 105 points, beating them by 30 and in the process handing Lute Olson
his worst loss as an Arizona coach.

After the game we couldn't have been happier. We had done exactly what
we wanted. We were 2-0 in the conference and undefeated at home after what
is always a tough weekend. Most importantly, we were starting to realize our
potential as a team. We had faced adversity that could've derailed a season,
and had not only overcame it, but recognized that we were getting better.
After the weekend we knew that the excitement would need to be short-lived.
After a home game against a struggling Morris Brown, both Arizona schools
would be anxiously awaiting our arrival the next week.

VISITING ABUSED CHILDREN

After Christmas the coaches arranged for us to go visit a center for
abused children outside Eugene. It was something, to be honest, at the time we
all thought of as taking time out of our schedule. I know that sounds like a
horrible thing to say, but I think that is how people are today — they look at
something from the standpoint of what is this going to cost me. We value any
free time and didn't realize the significance of the experience, I think we all
thought we were going to fulfill some public relations need.

However, I can't tell you how wrong we were. In fact I believe that this
was one of the experiences that helped us find out who we were as a basketball
team. The best part about it is that I don't think that the majority of the
members of the team made the connection at the time. It was the kind of
experience that brings about a subtle change.

Sometimes that's how change happens; you don't realize it until it has
already happened. It is human nature to be concerned about one's self.
However, I have found that it's when we are able to go against what is natural
and often times comfortable that we realize the most growth.

Each team is made up of individuals who want to do their best, which is putting it lightly, and sometimes those things make it hard to find out how they fit into the grand scheme of what the team is trying to accomplish. Our team was no different. However, something changed the day we made the drive out there, something we all felt but couldn't put a thought together that would match the feelings.

The property the center sits on is all but amazing. It's acres of riverside land overlooking a beautiful valley. We decided to carpool out to what seemed like a two-hour drive there, but in reality was a 25-minute drive back. When we arrived, we all drove up this extremely steep driveway that led to this huge house at the top of the hill. The director came out and, as we all stood on the porch, he told us the stories of some of the children in the home.

Reality set in immediately. The stories were horrifying, about every form of abuse you could think of. We had no idea what we were doing out there until this point. What seemed like a P. R. plan quickly turned into something more serious than basketball.

After the stories we had no idea what to expect. I envisioned the worst, and I don't think I was alone. We were given a quick tour and every eye in the room was upon us. Some of the cutest kids in the world stared at us. My first thought was, 'how could anyone have done the things that had been done to these little kids.' It was not difficult to see that they had missed out on some of the joys of being a child, something the center and its counselors where trying to fix.

We worked our way down to the lower-level deck just in time to catch the sunset while the director prepared the kids to officially meet us. As we all stood out there, for one of the very few times, our team was quiet, I am not sure exactly what others thought, but I will never forget my own thoughts. I was ashamed. Why? Without being to dramatic, because I had been so selfish that day. It's easy to get caught up in all that playing basketball at a high level involves. Sometimes you forget that the world goes on without you.

As we all stood there I quickly realized that evening's experience was more for us than for those kids for they had already been humbled, unfortunately without having a say in it. We, on the other hand, had not.

We were taught an important lesson that night…giving of ourselves, even if it hurts, even if you feel that it isn't necessary, even if you don't know why. This was something I feel we carried onto the floor, probably not even being aware of it, from that point on. We had talked before the season about becoming a team and the many things that requires, but sometimes it takes an experience like we had just had to have an impact.

As a team your goal is to become a group that not only believes in one another, but a family where each person unconditionally gives part of themselves to help reach the goals of the team. There is no difference in the size of the contribution. It only matters that it helps the team, whether it be someone giving up their points, their pride, their time to give support, or even if it means someone going the extra mile, giving more than they knew they could.

This is what a team is all about. It's easy to assemble a team full of talented players, especially if you have the name Duke, Cincinnati, or Kansas, but the difficult part is assembling a team whose players will give up something important of themselves for the team's success.

That night we learned not how to sacrifice for the team, but instead how to sacrifice for another. Once you have been taught this, the application is the easy part. Whether those kids remember our faces, I know we will never forget theirs or the lesson that they taught us that evening.

After we stood outside for a few minutes, we were led into a giant playroom, complete with a 30-foot tree, and, of course, a basketball hoop.

The kids were scattered around the room playing with their Christmas gifts as though it was the first time they had ever celebrated the holiday. I think they were as nervous as we were, but after a few minutes we warmed up to each other and ended up spending about an hour signing posters and playing games. On our way out the doors, it was clear that it was a valuable experience and something that would be on our minds for more than the drive back to Eugene.

ROUND 2

Our next game was a blowout against Morris Brown, a team that was in the process of moving up from Division II to Division I. They had struggled up until our game, and we didn't cut them slack, sending them home two days after Christmas with a 46-point loss. After brilliant shooting in the game against Arizona, we picked up right where we had left off, shooting 50 percent from the field, and using a balanced attack from every player on offense in route to a 96-50 victory.

After the game not much needed to be said. We all knew that the next seven days would be crucial to our goal of becoming PAC-10 champions. Two losses and our home wins a week earlier would have been all for naught. We had a seven-day layoff between the Morris Brown game and the Arizona game that would be played on a Friday instead of Thursday. This was because of a television conflict with the Rose Bowl that was played on that Thursday. Apparently somebody felt that it might be tough to get people to watch an Arizona-Oregon game instead of the National Championship football game. Go figure.

That week in practice there was an emphasis on staying sharp. Our team had really started to tap into its potential and the coaches wanted to make sure that we continued to get better, something that became our focus every day in practice.

The Arizona trip is always a fun trip. Up until that point we usually haven't played in a place that sees a lot of sun that time of the year. Because of the winter rain in Eugene, it's a welcome change for four days. Another good part of the trip is the food. We always eat at some great restaurants, and the Phoenix and Tucson areas have some good ones.

In the time between our first meeting and second, Arizona had been host of the Fiesta Bowl Tournament in Tucson. In one of the tournament games, Luke Walton had injured his foot and was questionable for our game. We assumed that Arizona was trying to make the injury sound worse than it was, and Walton would limp on to the floor, like Willis Reed. Our game plan included Walton playing. The coaches figured that it couldn't hurt to prepare for Arizona's best line-up.

The focus before the game seemed to be at a high level. There were a few games during the year were I would sit on the bench before the game and had no idea if we were ready to play. This was one of those games. Our warm-ups went well and the guards shot the ball well in the drills, but my concern was not so much our team as much as theirs. If Arizona got going at home, the Wildcats would be hard to beat, I felt our team was better than Arizona's was, but at that point in the season we seemed like we were just discovering our potential.

The McKale Center is, I feel, one of the toughest arenas in the league behind ours. It holds 16,000 fans, and they all dress in red and blue. Once the ball is tipped-off the crowd stands on its feet until the opponent's team scores. In 1999, we were up by seven points, and a guy went down onto the floor during a time-out with a sign that read, "stand until we have the lead." I remember seeing this and thinking confidently that they would be standing for a long time. Within about three minutes, the crowd was sitting, and we were trying to come from behind. In the McKale Center when it rains it pours, and it seems to rain a lot on visiting teams.

We hadn't won in Tucson since 1985. That's 17 years. We had a few guys on our team who were only a couple of years old when that game took place. The past two years, we had self-destructed each time we played there. In 1998, the year before I arrived, Oregon had a chance to win the game with a pair of Freddie Jones free throws, but Freddie missed both. The result was a two-point loss, something Freddie admitted he struggled with for a long time. Needless to say, Arizona was one of the tougher places to play.

Before the game everyone was quiet; the magnitude of the game had started to set in. It would be a sellout, and the fans expected their home team, which had knocked-off, Florida, Illinois and eventual National Champion Maryland earlier in the year, to get back into the winning grove after an ugly loss and a few close games in between. On the other hand we knew that nobody expected us to win, except for the 20 guys in the locker room. As odd as it sounds, that seemed to help us focus even more, something I later realized was the cause of the quiet locker room. We had begun to realize that in order to reach our goals we would have to be more focused and prepared than ever before. This was a characteristic that had begun to take shape, especially in our floor leaders, Freddie, Luke, and Luke.

The visitors' locker room at the McKale Center looks like an old P. E. locker room from high school. It has a few rows of lockers, and then an isolated open ceiling room with a dry erase board. As usual coach had the entire board covered with the game plan and reminders. After about 20 minutes of shooting and position meetings, we all met in the locker room.

"Since I have been at Oregon we have never brought a team down here that was the better team," Coach said. "This is no longer the case; tonight we have the better team," he finished as everyone shook their heads agreeing. There were times when you'd feel like you couldn't get any more excited to play, and then Coach would find a way to do it, even if it sounded a little corny.

I don't think anyone remembered what he said after that, but it didn't really matter. He was right; we were the better team. The key was to go out not just realizing that, but playing like that. Earlier in the year we had run into trouble. We had realized that we were a good team, but for a few games we forgot we had to show it in our play, something those losses certainly taught us.

WILDCATS

Whenever the home team's announcer announces the visiting team's starting line-up, he is as fast, monotone and unexciting as humanly possible. However, when it comes to the home team which is always announced last, the announcer makes it sound like he's Michael Buffer, "the let's get ready to rumble" guy. Arizona was no exception. It took as long to announce their point guard Jason Gardner as it did our entire starting line-up. To make matters worse, whenever they announced a player they would play this horrible cat growling noise, "RRRaaaaaRRRR," apparently it was supposed to sound like a wildcat. Unfortunately this noise was also played after just about everything the announcer said throughout the course of the game.

If someone scored a basket, the player's name would be announced, followed by the annoying "RRRaaaaaRRRR." It got so ridiculous that "the voice" came on one time to make an announcement for the concession stands that was immediately followed with "RRRaaaaaRRRR." By halftime I started to think Arizona had a guy at the scorer's table whose only job was to push a giant button that let out the horrible sound.

As usual tip-off brought the entire crowd on its feet. The pace of the game had picked up right where we had left of in Eugene. It was an up and down game that featured an array of poor shots on Arizona's part. Walton sat in street clothes at the end of the bench, his foot too sore for him to play. It looked like their entire team was trying to make up for his absence by playing better than the first game. There was one problem, we were playing just as well, Luke Ridnour was putting on a three-point shooting clinic, and Freddie was once again suffocating Gardner on defense. Robert Johnson, who was the unsung hero the entire year, was doing what he did best, playing defense and rebounding.

Without missing much of a beat we headed into the locker room up 11 points. The locker room was buzzing. We didn't think it would be this easy again. We had expected their best game, however, again failing to realize that it wasn't so much what they were doing as it was our execution and defense. This was something that we had yet to learn, up until that point the focus was equally upon them as it was us.

"One more half," Coach said as he strolled into the locker room knowing more than any of us that the game was far from over. For the next 10 minutes the focus was on taking care of business in the second half. We knew that the worst thing we could do was go out for the second half thinking they would just roll over for us.

The second half featured a lot of the same, Rid was on fire, and the Arizona players were still struggling to score.

"Not only did they not miss open shots, but they didn't miss shots when there was a lot of pressure on them," Olson said after the game.

Along with hitting 6-of-8 from the three-point line, Rid dished out 10 assists, Jackson dropped 21 and Freddie was beginning to be as consistent offensively and defensively as he had ever been. They made a few runs, but we answered every run with a huge shot. There was one play in the corner when they had put together a string of baskets and cut the lead. Rid got the ball, made a shot fake, took one dribble through his legs sending the defender off-balance, then finally brought the ball back to his shooting pocket before letting what looked like a carefree three from the corner go before the defender could get back off the ground. It went through the net with ease. The play seemed like a New York City playground move; the crowd let out a sigh and the game was all but over.

Continuing the playground style, Rid flew down the floor. Noticing Freddie out of the corner of his eye, it seemed like he was going to dribble right out of bounds on the baseline. Then at the last minute, he threw the ball off the backboard to a trailing Fred who caught the ball with two hands before flushing it down for a 22-point lead. The play was followed by a number of Oohs and Ahhs from none other than the Arizona faithful. They sensed that they were watching more than just a talented basketball team.

The game never felt close. With the exception of a three-pointer by Arizona guard Will Bynum in the final 30 seconds, the win would have been the worst home defeat at Arizona for Lute Olson. In fact the last time that the Wildcats had lost to a team at home by double digits was a 10-point loss in 1995 to UCLA, a team that went on to win the national championship. More importantly than just an impressive win, we had our first road victory of the year.

The locker room was surprisingly calm. It felt great to get a big win, but we realized that we still had one more win to get the sweep and be in control of the conference after the first two weeks. The most exciting thing about the win was the historical significance. We were beginning to realize that in order to become a prominent program we would need to erase records like being winless in Tucson for 17 years. It's a great stat to break, but not a great stat to have as a program.

The day after the game was spent traveling from Tucson to Phoenix. We woke up, got on the bus, and drove straight to Arizona State's Wells Fargo Arena for a light practice. The coaches knew that the game was going to be physical and we would need all the rest we could get. After practice we put our bags in our rooms and were told to meet down at the pool.

Our team trainer Clay met us at the pool. He informed us that we would be doing some cold water therapy that was designed to re-energize our legs.

Coach Radcliff, the strength and conditioning coach, had done some similar things with the football team during two-a-days. Clay was taking the whole thing pretty seriously, but we were acting like it was an MTV spring break. It was the first time we had really been in the sun, not to mention in a swimming pool. Guys were throwing each other around, trying to dunk big Chris, and tackling each other. Meanwhile Clay was trying to get everyone to do the exercises. Needless to say it wasn't easy. Who knows if it really worked? Neither Clay nor the coaches on any other trips brought up doing the exercises again. I can only imagine why?

The best part about playing the same teams in a two-week period is that preparation is not as grueling. Everyone still remembered their plays and what they tried to do. We knew that the Sun Devil coaches felt they had exposed a weakness and would be attacking us defensively off the dribble. To counter this we decided to give their players more room and encourage the outside shot. After all they hadn't shot the ball well, and the only reason they got the score back to a respectable margin at our place was because of getting to the basket and either scoring or getting fouled.

Playing at Wells Fargo Arena is not the most exciting experience. The place is hardly ever even half full. However, compared to past seasons, the crowd was a bit larger, and before the game the student section was actually rowdy. Someone told me that the students actually had to pay to get into their games. It started to make sense why they had so very few students attend. However, the few that did show that day seemed intent on getting their money's worth.

"Hey, Lindquist, how much did your dad pay to get you on the team," one student barked out. For some reason I was constantly harassed by other crowds. They always had the bland "you suck" for guys like Freddie, and Luke, and would regularly have a repetitious size joke for Chris, but for some reason the guys on the bench got the creative ones.

My sophomore year our first conference game was against Oregon State, and Kristian and I decided to shoot around a little early. We hadn't played OSU yet so I was surprised when I was immediately greeted with, "Hey, Lindquist and Christensen, which Back Street Boys are you supposed to be?" from the student section.

The Arizona State students always made up for their lack of numbers with their creativity. After taking a few more shots during warm-ups came, "Hey, Frat-boy, do you really think you're getting in?" I didn't play the last game and never really knew when Coach Kent would put me in, so I honestly replied, "Probably not." This seemed to catch them off-guard, but ended up only provoking them.

At the other end the Arizona State players looked ready to go. They appeared a little too confident after the way we had handled them just two weeks ago. We noticed this, and were determined to go out and try and beat them by even more.

The game started and we seemed to be a step slow. This time they were the ones who jumped out to an early lead. As he had in the Portland game, Freddie picked up a few fouls. The Sun Devils got an early lead by doing exactly what they had done the last 10 minutes of the game in Eugene, penetrating off the dribble. They were scoring in transition, and from the free throw line. Before the game they had appeared confident, and our passive play only contributed to that.

Fed up with the style of play and the score, Coach Kent started subbing. This was a common occurrence with Coach Kent; he had done this several times to try and provide a spark.

Out of nowhere I heard my name, but didn't move until he said it again, "Ben, go." I jumped up, a little surprised, and ran to the scorer's table. He had always juggled my playing time and this was something I had come to accept. Without thinking much about it I ran onto the floor to jeers form the student section. With about five minutes left in the first half the score was tied and we had gotten our energy back.

ASU was on a fast break when someone threw up a wild shot from the right baseline. It grazed the backboard and came off to the left side were I was waiting. Not realizing there was someone behind me I jumped up and caught an Arizona State elbow square on the nose. A little dazed, I went to the floor. Realizing I hadn't gotten the rebound I jumped back up and felt something running down my face. I assumed it was sweat, brushed it off, and realized it was blood. By this time the blood had really started to flow. I thought maybe my nose was broken, so I turned to the ref on the baseline and gave him a, "can't you tell I'm bleeding?" look. A little surprised himself, he blew his whistle and Clay brought a towel onto the floor.

I found myself on the bench with a towel over my face, and asked Clay if my nose was on the other side of my face. My nose had been broken several times before – my only excuse for its large size — and this seemed to hurt worse than any previous break.

Clay pulled the towel off and, to my surprise, told me there was a cut. He asked me if I wanted to get stitched up and try and play the second half, or to sit out and wait until after the game.

Of course I wanted to play, so we headed to the training room. On my way out I had to pass the student section, where its members had satisfied looks on their faces.

I got to the training room, and was met by the Arizona State team doctor. My parents just happened to be at the game, and also joined me.

After getting seven stitches in my nose I tried to stand up and see if I really wanted to keep playing. I looked over at the doctor and kept thinking he looked familiar. Then my dad said the same thing out loud. After a few minutes of tracing personal history, the three of us remembered we had played golf together. The doctor and my dad had even exchanged business cards about six years earlier at a lakeside resort town in northern Utah.

My thoughts however, quickly turned to the game. I wanted to win so badly, a broken nose seemed worth the price. However, a loss didn't feel like an acceptable trade-off for a painful couple of weeks.

At the half we were down 44-41, and we thought we had weathered the storm. After some simple checks to make sure I was coherent enough to play, I headed back down to the floor, again passing the student section, which now had pieces of tape on their noses, mocking the similar piece on my own nose.

We had slipped behind even more. I think of all the games this was the strangest. We just couldn't consistently keep anything going.

After a few minutes of sitting on the bench I was again put into the game. We cut the lead again, but still couldn't get over the hump. My nose had started to bleed and I had to come out of the game again. Arizona State was in control of the game and everything we tried to do was ineffective. Freddie had fouled out and we made a valiant push at the end, but we never really threatened. This time is was our team that couldn't get a basket and their team that was getting all the stops on the defensive end. The result: a 95-88 loss, and a 3-1 record in the PAC-10.

Coach Graham stormed in the locker room, yelling about the way the end of the game played out. He was upset that we had shot some ill-advised threes in the final minute. I think the real frustration was that we were in such a good position and let a chance to get through a difficult part of the schedule 4-0 get away. Coach Kent added a little bit to that and abruptly finished. We hung our heads as we teamed it up.

As the rest of the team went out to dinner, I headed to get X-rays, finding out that my nose was broken. But it appeared to be a clean break and hopefully wouldn't require any surgery. I went out to dinner feeling like someone had taped a brick to my face. I don't know if it was the pain from the nose or the loss that hurt worse, but there weren't a whole lot of smiles from anybody. We met that night. Coach had a chance to calm down, and had already switched gears to the critical weekend at home just four days away against the Bay Area schools.

DON'T GET TOO HIGH OR TOO LOW!

Coach Kent often talked about not getting too high or too low. This was in reference to winning and losing and the fine line between the behavior after each. He was actually a pretty good example of this. After a gut-wrenching loss, he never over-reacted. Not that he didn't get upset, but he never took it to the extremes that many coaches often do. When we won a big game he would immediately mention the fact that we should enjoy the victory for the night, but remember our biggest game was the next one and not to look any shorter or any farther. The things Coach would say after a loss always surprised me. He always seemed to have a good feel for the emotional state of the team, and realized our team took every loss hard.

The day after the Arizona State game Coach was upbeat and at his best, spinning the loss the day before into a positive for the future. He wanted to make sure we didn't forget the win against Arizona, and the importance it had for not just our team, but for the program. He spoke of learning how to win on the road and how the trip forced us to be mentally stronger. He was already talking about the games that week, and how Cal and Stanford would be a test. Coach had put the loss to Arizona State behind him, and expected us to do the same.

Robert Johnson, one of Oregon's most solid players ever.

CHAPTER 5
Oh, the places you'll go...

"Success is never final.
Failure is never fatal.
It is the courage that counts"
— *Winston Churchill*

Each game was getting bigger and bigger. We were only four games into conference play, and we were already facing weekends in which getting swept could easily mean knocking us out of contention, especially with as much balance as the conference had. Cal and Stanford are always a difficult series, Cal slows the game down to a snail's pace, and Stanford forces you to be accountable on every possession. Coming into the game all the talk was about Cal's defense and how the Bears kept their opponent's scoring around 60 points per game, well below the 80's we had been averaging.

We, of course, knew that the particular statistic being proudly discussed was misleading. The reason that Cal was able to keep the score so low was because its players used the entire shot clock the majority of the time. Against us we knew they would be doing whatever they could to keep the score low in hopes of throwing off our high-powered fast break.

Our goal that week was to get the sweep, something Oregon hadn't accomplished since Coach Kent had been here. The media was still talking about how maybe Arizona was over-rated, and that we had simply put together a few good games. However, talk of a PAC-10 championship was just that, talk. We knew that if we were going to have any shot at winning the conference title we would have to get both games that weekend. If we succeeded, the conference would be chasing us.

The Cal game was a typical conference game, back and forth. Cal came out ready to play, but we were just as ready, especially after a disappointing start to the last game. It was back and forth through the entire first half. We were playing hard, but not getting the regular breaks.

At the half the game was tied at 30-30, a score that the Cal players probably felt good about. At the half Coach was especially positive. We had battled hard, and he knew that at some point in the second half the Bears would break.

The second half was hard-fought. Cal was playing well, and we were playing just good enough to stay in the game. Coming down the stretch, we started to make our move. The entire game the Cal players hadn't seemed comfortable with the lead, and, with a few minutes remaining we took advantage of that. Freddie and Anthony were the only guys who were really hitting, Luke and Luke were struggling from the field, but doing the little things as usual. Big Chris was having a solid game, getting into double figures and starting to provide an inside presence.

There really wasn't one single play that changed the face of the game. It just seemed like the Bears started to get rattled. The whole game they had held their composure, but, with about three minutes left, they began to lose it. It was the little things in this game; we started to get the stops, and got a few big baskets. However, the feel of the game was different from others. So far in the season there had usually been a big play that had either started a run or ended that of another team. This game seemed like we were creeping up on them one play at a time until they got uncomfortable and started to make little mistakes, like bad shots, and ill-advised fouls.

The game would come down to free throws, and, by the time the game was over, we had a 76-72 come from behind win. The whole game was bizarre; they shot a better percent than us from the field, and the three-point line. They had more assists and almost half as many turnovers, 10 compared to our 18. Every statistic that is important to winning was in their favor, yet we came away with the victory. When we got into the locker room, everyone looked around wondering how we had just won a game where we not only played poorly, but the opponent had played well.

"I'm telling you right now," Coach started in, "it's your defense that will win you games."

The question in every one's face had just been answered. We had won the first three games of the conference with outstanding offensive performances mixed with flashes of defense. However, we had just won our fourth game almost solely on defense. The whole time Litz sat in the back, finally starting to see the fruits of his and our labor.

We learned a valuable lesson from that game. It was not a lesson about life or about relationships; it was a basketball lesson. Defense can win games! Sure everyone talks about Defense winning championships. In fact, that very phrase has sat in 12-inch letters on the wall in the team room at Mac Court for a number of years.

Growing up every player hears it. But that night we didn't just see it first hand in a game we would have lost by 20 the year before, but we also started to believe it as a team. On a team with so many great offensive players, we started to believe we could win games with more than three-pointers and dunks. We had known all year the importance of defense, but the difference was now every player believed it.

As usual, rest and preparation was the coaches' highest priority, so the next day we had a light practice with the majority of the time spent on

Stanford's number of offensive plays. Stanford was coming off a win against Oregon State, and both teams expected a close game.

Not one player on the team had ever beaten Stanford, home or on the road. Similar to Arizona, coach wanted to make sure that we knew we were the better team. Deep down I think Coach Kent wanted to beat Stanford more than anybody. He had coached there as an assistant under Mike Montgomery and every coach wants to beat the guy he coached under, almost as a sign that he is making a name for himself.

In the past Stanford had beaten us with its size and execution. The last two years we were in a position to win at home and lost in the final minutes. However, with the departure of the Collins twins to the NBA, Stanford was a much different team than in the past. A big part of our success would involve stopping all-American guard Casey Jacobsen and future NBA big man Curtis Borchardt. Other than that the Cardinal really couldn't hurt you in a lot of other areas.

The pace of the game started in our favor. We were able to get a few easy baskets, and everyone seemed to be on his game, including big Chris who was a big part of how well we did against bigger teams. Chris seemed particularly active to start the game, and, when he was out, Brian Helquist came in and was just as solid.

The game was starting to slip away from Stanford when Casey Jacobsen began to heat up. When you play against a great player, especially a shooter, defensively the most important thing is limiting the easy baskets. This becomes frustrating and usually leads to forced shots that end up playing into your hands.

Casey had started the game determined to get his team going. Unfortunately he had Luke Jackson defending him well. Before the game, our plan was to try and take the ball out of his hands as much as possible. If he were to get the ball and pass it, we would immediately take him out as soon as the ball was passed, similar to a face-guarding defense from junior high.

This was working great to start the game. We were forcing other players to try and make the plays that their best player usually made. We knew he would score, but we wanted to make him work for every shot. Jacobsen got the ball at the top of the three-point line and took a dribble to his left. While trying to guard him, Luke Jackson slipped. Casey recognized this instantaneously, took one dribble to get his balance, and fired in an NBA three. It had started. He got the look in his eyes, and we knew that he would be trying even harder to get his shots.

The first half was back and forth; Luke Jackson also had the look in his eyes, and was on his way to a team high in points. At halftime we held a six-point lead, which probably should have been 10. The locker room was very positive. We knew we had a lot of time left, but we also felt like the Cardinal was ripe for the picking. If we could just stop Jacobsen and limit Borchardt, who had also knocked down a few jumpers, then we knew we'd win the game.

In the second half Luke Jackson was hitting from just about everywhere, on the fast break, jumpers, and at the foul line. For a stretch it looked like a one-on-one battle between him and Jacobsen. For the first time in the three years I'd played against Stanford, Jacobsen had shown signs of frustration. There were a few plays he thought Jackson had fouled him and this only seemed to give Luke even more confidence.

Along with Luke, Chris was having one of his better games of the year, scoring 16 points and uncharacteristically shooting 6-of-7 from the foul line. Everyone else was solid. Freddie scored at the right time, and Luke was controlling the tempo of the game. On the defensive end, we were stopping just about everyone except the two guys we needed to stop. Jacobsen was scoring just enough to keep them in the game, and Borchardt was making enough jumpers to keep it an uncomfortably close game.

With a three-point Oregon lead in the final minute, Stanford called a timeout and set up a play for Jacobsen. The year before we were in the final minutes of the game and he had gotten the ball in the far corner right in front of the student section, set his feet and knocked down a game-breaking three-pointer. In the timeout we knew exactly who the Cardinal was going to have shoot — Jacobsen. They set up what looked like the same play, and there Jacobsen was all alone in the corner. The ball immediately went to the corner, and, as Jacobsen set his feet he took his eye of the ball for a split second. The result, the ball squirted through his hands and went out of bounds.

Everyone in the building took a double take; Casey himself even looked surprised. As the ball was heading out of bounds he tried hopelessly to save it, stumbling forward, finally regaining his balance with a look that said it all, Stanford had broken. The Stanford that for so many years had dominated us, had finally broken first. Although there was still time on the clock the game was over, and everyone in the gym including the Stanford players knew it.

THE KARATE DANCE

My first year we won quite a few close games. An Arizona State game that we won at the buzzer was probably one of the most exciting games I had ever been a part of. After the game the team traditionally meets for about 10 minutes. Coach Kent is usually the last one to arrive. He waits until everyone is seated and gathers his thoughts before coming in and talking.

After the ASU game we all ran down to the locker room. Everyone was yelling and jumping around in excitement, waiting for Coach to come into the room. When I got into the team room I was so excited I started to mimic karate moves from a class I had taken as a kid. Of course, it wouldn't be complete unless I threw in some Bruce Lee sound effects to finish the job. The team watched for about a minute as I embarrassed myself, and I finally stopped when I became a little dizzy.

This little dance started to become a tradition after big wins. However, the following season it disappeared because of a lack of those big wins that had propelled us to the NCAA tournament. It was one of those things that you don't decide to do until it's the right moment. For example you wouldn't jump up and do the "Karate Dance" after beating lowly Morris Brown.

THE REVIVAL

As we headed down to the locker room while the fans stormed the court, I thought of the ASU game of two years past. We were all sitting in the team room and I suddenly found myself in the front of the room with my back to the team. I began to turn around and step one foot at a time like a sumo wrestler. I came to a stop and the "Karate Dance" was reborn. After about a minute of moving around the room like Mr. Meuagi, I finally sat down. Out of breath I looked over at Jay; he was shaking his head in disbelief, "Don't ever do that again," he said. This, of course, meant he thoroughly enjoyed the entire thing.

Coach Kent walked in as the laughter and excitement of the game was finishing, and asked what had been going on. I simply told him "the Karate Dance." The next day he asked me when he'd see the "Karate Dance." I told him only a big win will decide. In my mind I was secretly planning on the next game at Stanford, another place like Arizona where Oregon hadn't won since the mid-80's.

After things had settled down, the room went silent. Everyone looked around the room, and there was a sense of satisfaction; we were 5-1, and the possibilities had begun to be realized. We had talked about winning the PAC-10 championship, but for the first time it felt like we were actually doing it, even if it was game by game.

No one was prouder than Coach; you could tell the win meant a lot to him. "You're getting better," he said. "This is starting to feel like one of those magical rides, and, if you can continue to buy into what we are teaching, who knows where this thing will end up?" Each player nodded his head. Without wanting to jinx ourselves, we had begun to realize that this year was going to be different; I sat and thought for a minute, Oh, the places we'll go!

75TH ANNIVERSARY

As a team we were excited for the 75th anniversary of Mac Court. The building has been home to so many great games over a 75-year span. As a team we loved Mac Court. For every guy on the team, part of the reason they came had to do with Mac Court. In a day where the state-of-the-art arena is the norm, Mac Court has an old school feel that is hard to describe. The love for Mac Court comes not just from the games, but the time spent alone on the floor. I can remember a number of times sitting at halfcourt all alone at night just looking around, wondering what it must have been like years ago. The building has a magical feel to it. Whether it's the miniature Boston Garden look or the bizarre cemetery across the street, Mac Court is certainly not your average college basketball arena. "The PIT" as it is known, was proclaimed as the best gym in college basketball by The Sporting News. And Sports Illustrated rated it the toughest place to play in the PAC-10. You could probably write a book just about all the great games and memories that the historic building has held.

The first game played in Mac Court featured Oregon against Willamette. So, in the spirit of the anniversary the athletic department decided to play against the same opponent 75 years to the day from that same day. The honorary captain for the game was Ret. Admiral John Dick, who had led his team in scoring on its way to the first basketball national championship ever.

We all knew, including the players from Willamette, that the game would not be close. However, we wanted to not only celebrate Mac Court, but also to avoid any injury or slippage in the progress we had made during the confer-

The Historic Mac Court.

ence season. For Willamette the game provided a chance for a Division III school whose players probably never played in front of more than a couple thousand fans an opportunity to play in Mac Court, in front of 10,000 fans. The majority of the players on the Willamette roster were from Oregon, so it meant a lot to play Oregon in Mac Court.

In the spirit of remembering history, we decided as a team to ask Coach Kent about wearing our socks higher than usual, and even briefly threw around the idea of throw-back era uniforms, with the old school gold and green. We came away from the negotiations with permission to wear the higher socks, and didn't feel like testing our limits with any other requests.

The day of the game we all showed up with ridiculously high socks that looked straight out of the 70's. Coach Kent made it clear that this would be a one-time deal, and after seeing how absurd those high socks looked on my legs, I wasn't too disappointed.

During the introductions, the crowd gave a cheer as loud as ours when the Willamette players were introduced, another testament to not only their knowledge of the game, but also a respect. The game was never really close, but it was never really a blowout. Willamette came out determined to prove that it could hang with a bigger school, and for the first 15 minutes did so! Without disrespecting a team that fought and played hard, the focus was more about honoring a great building and the loyal fans who had been coming to the games for 75 years than it was about us going out and wanting to beat them by 50 points. Our focus was to play through the game and get in some conditioning. Coach Kent made it clear that he wanted us to play hard and use the game as a conditioning tool. If we didn't do that, he also made it clear that he would take care of the conditioning the next few days.

The game was never pretty; it included a lot of sloppy play and poor execution. The result a 71-48 victory that wouldn't count as an NCAA win because of Willamette's Division III status. As foolish as it sounds, it didn't really feel like there were any losers. Willamette had played hard and was even effective at times, not to mention its players all looked like they had a great time in front of a crowd that cheered their success just as much as ours. We escaped without any injuries, and everyone played. In the back of our minds we knew we were in the middle of something more important, a championship run.

THE CIVIL WAR

After six games we were in the title hunt. It sounded a little early to get excited about something that far away, but for the bottom four teams, ideas of the conference title were already being dumped for hopes of just getting into the conference tournament. One of those schools was Oregon State. At 1-5 the Beavers were in the middle of a rebuilding process that had been going on for a number of years, and also fighting to beat out Washington and Washington State for the eighth spot. With a win against us, they would not only win bragging rights around the state, but also be in a great spot to distance themselves from the Washington schools that were winless at that point in the conference.

For us this was a must-win; a loss and we might as well have split the previous week. If we couldn't beat the teams in the lower half of the conference, there was no way we were going to have a shot at the title or the NCAA tournament.

It had been three years since Oregon State had won a Civil War game. The Civil War was beginning to lose its flavor. In my three years we had won by an average of about 17 points. It was kind of ironic; the game was important to both schools, but for different reasons, for us it was to stay in title contention, for them it was to stay out of the last two spots of the conference.

Oregon State had made some improvements from the previous season, and much like Cal had resorted to slowing the game down. Having the first game at home would help give the Beavers even more of a chance to control the speed of the game.

When you play your travel partner, the game is usually on a Saturday. This gives each school a chance to either play a non-conference game during the week, or get some extra rest depending on its scheduling. With the Willamette game we had been able to do both. We had played early enough in the week that we still had plenty of time to prepare for OSU, and still get a day off.

The next day of practice was back to defense, Litz huddled us up and said, "There is one thing that every rivalry game comes down to, it's not who has the better record, or who is more talented. It's who plays defense!" When Litz spoke he was always passionate. He made you feel like you were in a scene from Hoosiers and the next play would decide the 1954 Indiana State Championship.

Coach didn't have to do a lot of coaching before the OSU game. It was never difficult to get ready to play our rival. In fact, Coach Kent always made sure he reminded us of the history the Civil War held. That week we turned up our intensity in practice even more. We had begun to taste success and wanted more of it. It was easy to notice the difference from just a year ago when our record was almost the exact opposite.

Every year on the bus ride to Corvallis, Coach buys a highlight video to play on the way up. This year he bought a NBA highlight video from the Hall of Fame gift shop. The videos were usually pretty good; last year he got the Michael Jordan IMAX video, which everybody thought was pretty impressive. However, this year's video was a bit of a letdown. It was a mid-90's highlight video that had just about everything except highlights. After giving him a hard time about his video selection we arrived at the Gill Coliseum.

Gill Coliseum is a classic college basketball gym. It's open and there isn't a bad view in the place. The locker rooms are a different story. It takes about 10 minutes to get down to the locker rooms, after a number of stairs you feel like you're going to come out of the stairway and end up in China.

Most home teams stick the visitors in the worst locker room possible. This locker room was probably not the worst, but certainly not the best. I think it was the old visitor's locker room for the football stadium across the street. To get to the bathroom you have to go out two doors and down the hall. The bathrooms are so old the toilets don't even have doors on the stalls, needless to say only the new guys went the bathroom there because the veterans all planned ahead.

The game wasn't a sellout, but the arena was pretty full. We jumped out to an early lead with a few baskets from Robert Johnson, including a foul line jump shot that banked in. It was one of those shots where the coach is yelling, "don't shoot, don't shoot," then the shot goes up and surprisingly in and the coach quickly turns to, " great shot, great shot." In a game where controlling the tempo was OSU's whole game plan, we had seized control early. The first half our lead fluctuated between 10 and 15 points. Of all our games, this was probably one of the most balanced in terms of team scoring.

It was always interesting to see how each team would try and disrupt our system. Some teams would try and faceguard Rid so he couldn't get the outlet pass to start our fast break. Other teams would throw a full court press on us. Sometimes this played into our hands more than anything we could have done on the other end defensively. Having another team's best players use all of their energy trying to stop us on defense usually meant tired jump shots and slower first steps for them on offense. Whatever they tried seldom worked. Coach Kent prepares with the best of them, and in practice we probably worked more on playing against the changes teams would make than the actual teams spent on making those changes.

It wasn't hard to tell that there was a difference between our team and theirs. I think the crowd enjoyed watching our team more than their own, and it looked like the players were quietly wishing that they were running up and down the floor shooting threes and dunking with us instead of against us. Their style of play was so slow; at one point in the game I leaned over to James and said, "No wonder why they hardly get any fans to the game, I wouldn't pay to watch this either."

Without saying so, I felt like my high school team was probably more exciting to watch. Every once in a while a player would take the ball, go one-on-one and throw up a wild shot, almost as a signal that he was going crazy in a system that seldom fast breaks and plays a half-court game the entire time. The irony was that this was the time that the crowd was most excited, something that by the time the season was over led to a new coach and hopes of a new style of play.

Meanwhile we had adjusted our style of play to the pace of the game. We were an up-and-down-the-floor type of team, but we knew they wanted to slow the game down. So our game plan was to be patient and not force any poor shots in frustration. We did exactly that, with the exception of a few shots in the first half; we found ourselves playing an entirely different style and being successful. Oregon State stayed within that same 10-15 point margin for the second half, threatening a couple of times before running out of enough shots and defense.

The game ended neither as a close game nor a blow out, but instead a 12-point road victory. We had a few chances to make it a 20-point game, but we also realized that we had won a game that forced us to grow as a team on the floor. By playing a half-court game where each possession is important, we were forced to either adapt to the pace of play or risk forcing things and making it a close game on the road. Also, our defense had showed another strong performance, again getting vital stops in the half-court; something we all knew would be the key to winning down the stretch. After the game everyone felt great; there aren't a lot of better feelings in sports than beating your rival. Regardless of each team's record, it always feels like a good win.

In an off-season where each week we'd grown as friends and teammates, each game in the season had begun to shape us into a basketball team. It felt like we were getting better each game, and our record had started to show it, 14-4, (6-1). With a road trip to Washington, we knew getting a sweep would put us in the drivers' seat at the halfway point, and give us even more confidence for a tough second half of conference play.

THE SPEED BUMP

We were rolling. We had won nine of our last 10, and after playing some of the tougher league opponents, we looked forward to the Washington trip as a chance to get a sweep and increase our title chances. Standing in our way were two Washington teams that had won one conference game between them.

The Washington road trip, believe it or not is one of our toughest. Every year the games are close. My first year the first game against UW was an overtime win, followed by a double-overtime win at WSU. Last year, the game with UW in Eugene was also an overtime contest. It seems that regardless of how good or bad their teams were, the games always seemed to be close.

Every time we played UW, the first thing Coach Kent would say is, "with the exception of OSU, Washington is our biggest rival." With the battles between the football teams and the overall dislike for each other's schools, any game between the two certainly had that feel. We didn't like them one bit, and we knew they wanted nothing more than to beat us.

Washington was a different type of team from those we had faced all year. For parts of games the Huskies had flashes of brilliance and, at other times, the look of disorder. They appeared to have talented players, but never seemed too sure of what they were trying to accomplish on the floor. They were athletic and fast, but also undisciplined, which can be a bad combination. Our game plan was similar to many others, limit their best players and let their worst players try and uncharacteristically beat us. Most importantly, though, was the focus on playing our game; something we knew, if done, would lead to a victory.

Travel to Seattle was uneventful. After a team meal, we headed to the hotel and to bed. It was always the longest road trip of the conference, and we needed to be rested. The day of the game was routine, but at the shoot-around we looked a little out of sync. Big Chris and Brian looked a little out of rhythm, but nothing that caused too much concern.

In the locker room before the game the focus was on nothing but beating UW. At tip-off the building was nearly full and loud. The game got off to a lightning pace; UW had jumped out on us and refused to back down. We looked a little surprised. They had come out like they were the team in the title hunt and we were the bottom-dweller. It felt like the Twilight Zone; they were fast breaking, dunking, making three-pointers, and we were making all the mistakes we try to force other teams to make. From bad shots and unforced turnovers to poor transition defense and being out-hustled, the roles had been reversed. At the half they had all the momentum and a 52-44 lead.

Before the coaches came in, the locker room was full of noise. We were all upset at the way we had played, and everyone was adding what they thought we needed to do differently. After a few minutes of this, the door opened and Coach Kent came in. The room went silent, "We are letting one guy beat us," Coach said, referring to their best player Doug Wren, who was on his way to a 30 point night. "We're not getting back in transition and were bailing them out with our turnovers and poor shots."

It seemed as though we had shown up with the idea of walking onto the court and having them give us the game. However, the first half was evidence that we would be going back to the hotel with a loss if we had another half like that.

When the second half started, it was right back to business. We started picking away at the lead, slowly getting the momentum back on our side. This time the Huskies were the ones surprised, apparently assuming we were going to hand them the game. Play continued to be close; they would take the lead, then we would crawl back, taking it a few more times. By this time the crowd had begun to get into the game and the overall intensity picked up even more.

In the final minutes the game felt as though it could go either way. When the horn sounded, we had somehow lost. There wasn't really a play that stood out, but instead the game had fallen through our fingers and it felt like we couldn't do anything about it. It didn't feel like one particular thing had lost us the game, but instead every part of the game. They had played well, and not that we played terrible, but for the first time in weeks we failed to do what had gotten us there, DEFEND!

After the game the locker room was uncomfortably silent; no one was awaiting the arrival of Coach Kent through the door. The door opened and, to our surprise, he too was silent. Waiting to put words together to match his thoughts, he stood in front of the team almost speechless, something he hardly ever is.

"First, I want to say that you did a great job of fighting back into the game." This however, was without comfort. We had all known we had blown it and we were only waiting for him to make it official.

Without saying much, he put his final thoughts on the game, summing up the reasons why we lost and finishing with, " Don't let them beat us twice. We still have to go to Pullman and make sure we have the same energy," referring to the importance of not letting the disappointing loss carry over into our next game. Before walking out the door to the media, he added, "We have started to become the hunted, and every team will get up to play us."

After the coaches wrapped up, we all sat there for a few minutes. The season had begun to feel like a roller coaster. We would work our way up each week getting better and better, feeling like we were finally getting to the top; and perhaps becoming a team worth placing the word champion next to.

Then, without warning, it felt like we were sent down the tracks on a 200-foot drop, wondering if it was the end of our championship ride or just the next hill to get over on our way to our goal.

Whichever it was, we knew we couldn't keep losing to the teams we should be beating, and the ones all the other title-contending teams were beating. Outside the doors of the locker room, the media was waiting, UW's players had already been running their mouths about how this was the game in which they finally turned the corner and how they knew they could beat us. Meanwhile everyone on our team was gracious, talking about how UW played well and deserved to win.

We realized that any disrespect would only be a disservice, but more importantly we had a game in Pullman that had now become a must win. After the cameras and tape recorders were gone, we knew we had given the game away, and couldn't wait to play them again.

PULLMAN

Pullman is definitely the worst place to play on the road. The trip there is especially bad. Pullman is about a one-hour plane ride from Seattle, but you never know if you're going to get there because of the weather. So, our coaches decided to fly to Spokane and drive to Pullman to avoid any delays bad weather might cause. Because Pullman doesn't have many hotels, we stay about 20 minutes away in Moscow, Idaho, not Russia, although we felt so far away from everything it could have been. I think the hotel we stay in is about 30 years old. I always got a kick out of the room Coach Kent stayed in. We usually had our team meetings in Coach's room. Most of the time it was a larger room that had some form of conference room feel to it. However, in this hotel the only room that fits that requirement is called the Presidential Suite. It is filled with 80's furniture and a lot of strangely placed mirrors. I always wondered why they needed a Presidential Suite in Moscow, Idaho. My only answer is that perhaps someone else got it confused with Russia too.

Along with the travel and the hotel, the WSU trip is the worst because of the game environment. In a conference full of historic and loud gyms, WSU is a hard place to get excited about. The arena itself is great. It probably holds around 14, 000 and is fairly modern, but the problem is the crowd. The announced attendance at our game was just over 3,000, and at that point was a season high. The top section of the arena is covered with plastic, and the seats underneath probably have a fresh coat of paint from just after the George Raveling days.

It feels like you're playing a game somewhere on the other side of the world that nobody cares about, including the majority of people in attendance. We were not apart of that group; this game meant a great deal to us. A loss and we lose ground that we might not be able to get back, a win and we start climbing right back up the hill again toward our goal.

The night before the game featured a meal at Applebee's, the nicest restaurant in town, and a movie. To make sure we all understood what was at stake there was a walk-through and a meeting that night in the Presidential Suite. The game featured an afternoon tip-off so we wouldn't have a chance to make the 20-minute drive there and back beforehand and still be able to get enough rest in-between.

The next morning we woke up, had breakfast and another walk-through to make sure we had no excuses. Coach Duncan, who is usually in charge of making sure the red-shirts who aren't eligible to play get a workout in, headed to the arena early, Anthony, Jay, and I decided to join them. When we arrived, there was a junior cheerleading clinic going on so we ended up sitting around and talking about potential ways the Cougars could get more fans to the games. My personal best was to give away free tickets.

After we had shot the breeze for about 45 minutes, the rest of the team showed up. We met in the locker room and began our usual pre-game routines. There wasn't a lot Coach Kent had to say; we all realized the importance of the game. He kept it simple, reminding us if we defended we'd win, something we had temporarily forgotten in Seattle.

When the game started there was about as much energy as 3,000 people in a 14,000-seat arena can generate. We controlled the game from the tip; Coach was subbing early, which was usually a signal that if you weren't playing hard then you would be pulled out. Coach Kent will usually sub until he finds a combination that works well. When he threw James in, he struck gold. James was particularly hot that day, finishing with a career-high 21 points. Rid continued his spectacular play with 24 points after scoring 23 two days earlier. At the half we had a comfortable 43-34 lead.

The second half featured a lot of the same, including a 20-point lead at one point. Just when Coach Kent was getting ready to clear the bench and finish the blowout, something started to happen. Marcus Moore, their best player had provided their only real spark, finally he caught fire, hitting three's left and right. When we took those away he started getting to the basket for lay-ups. For about a four-minute stretch he was unstoppable, a 25-point blowout had all of the sudden turned into a much closer game.

Luke Jackson, who was having a rare off game, got the ball on the left baseline and appeared to be out of room to make any plays. He picked up the ball and, after desperately looking around to pass, threw up a right-handed flip shot that somehow found a way into the basket, thus stopping the bleeding from the Marcus Moore assault. The Cougars managed to stay with us for a few more minutes until some critical foul shooting by James, Rid and Freddie sealed a 94-86 road win. The locker room was back to normal; we had gotten the split and half way through the conference were right back in the title hunt at 7-2. After a hitting a speed bump at Washington, we were headed back up the road to a championship.

It wasn't even 5 p.m. and we had plenty of time to celebrate. Because the game was early, we had two choices, charter a bus and drive straight back to Eugene, or bus to Spokane and spend the night before flying back to Eugene. By a split decision we decided to spend the night in Spokane.

This turned out to be a poor decision. That night we were excited about getting to Spokane, getting some dinner and hanging out. After a painless drive, we checked into a hotel that felt like the Ritz compared to the hotel in Moscow. We showered, changed and headed to dinner. While we waited in the lobby for everyone to meet, there happened to be a TV tuned to the Washington-Oregon State game. Apparently the corner the Washington players claimed the Huskies had turned after beating us had led to a dead end as they lost to Oregon State that night. Instead of bringing us satisfaction, that OSU victory only reminded us that we would have to pick up a game some-where down the stretch to make up for the loss.

Dinner is always more enjoyable when you win, and this night was no exception. We all had a good meal, then hung out at the hotel. About mid-night Luke Jackson, Jay, Matt Short and I decided to head down to the hot tub and indoor pool to pass some time. After telling stories about almost every-thing, we looked out the glass windows. At the fourth floor hall window was Coach Kent looking down at us. At that point it was about 1:30 a.m. We weren't really sure if he was going to be mad about us being up so late. Before we could think up excuses, he shook his head as though he thought the whole thing was pretty funny. We all broke into laughter at the awkward moment, not realizing how strange four guys in a hot tub in the middle of the night might look.

114

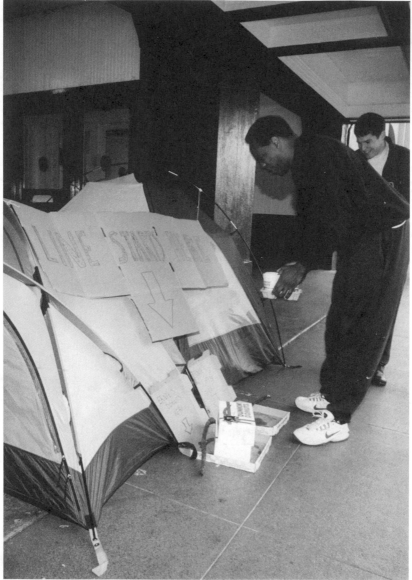

Coach Kent bringing food to the Mac Court faithful who camped over night to get seats to the game.

CHAPTER 6
The Midterm

"How you respond to the challenge in the second half
will determine what you will become after the game,
whether you are a winner or not." — Lou Holtz

In a season full of tests, we were halfway through the conference and ready
for our midterm, a home series against UCLA and USC. Six teams were chasing
the title with us. We were beginning to head into uncharted waters as a basketball
program. It had been years since Oregon had been mentioned with the words
"first place" halfway through the conference season. A win in the Thursday
game against UCLA would give us a two-game lead over the Bruins and a chance
for sole possession of first against USC on Saturday. At 15-5 and 7-2 in the
conference we had already won more games than we had the previous year. We
had also picked up two more conference victories in the first half of play than we
had in an entire conference season. We knew we were a better team than we had
been the previous year. At this point in the season we were beginning to
eliminate questions about the last season and start to raise questions about a
potential run at the title.

It had begun to feel like each week a loss meant a giant step back and a win
simply meant you stayed in the race for another week. The conference season is
certainly a marathon, but at the halfway point we were at the head of the pack.
We knew full well we had a lot farther to go before we started thinking about
anything beyond playing the next game. The coaching staff was doing a great

job of keeping the team loose. Our focus was the same every week — take it one game at a time and get better every day.

PRACTICE

The best way for us to get better every day was through practice. At this point in the season we took a day off after every Saturday game to make sure we had fresh legs for the following week. With a Sunday off, Monday was the day we usually went the hardest. Practice was usually full of some form of up-and-down the floor scrimmaging, including a lot of defensive work.

The defensive work stayed the same every week; Coach Litz was always given time in practice but certainly not enough to suit him. Each day we worked on our defensive fundamentals, Litz felt like late in the season was when the fundamentals slipped the most. He was determined not to let us off the hook, knowing full well that a commitment to defense had been one of the difference-makers. After a weekend in Washington where two players effortlessly scored 30 points on us, that week in practice was more about defense than anything else.

There was a lot of importance placed on practice because we had struggled with consistency on that end all the previous year. We couldn't go more than a week without a practice where Coach Kent didn't feel like kicking us out. Sometimes we'd even have a great first half of practice only to somehow find a way to go completely brain-dead by the end of the day. Our inconsistency had shown the entire season in both practice and games. Whether it was losing games we should have won or the up-and-down identity we brought to each game, we carried over poor practices to our games.

As "Spock" from Star Trek would say, "it's only logical," to eliminate carrying over poor practices into games, you need to eliminate poor practices. So every day that was our focus. By the end of the year we had only had two or three bad practices.

When we start practice each day, we gather around the "O" at halfcourt and stretch for about 10 minutes while Coach Kent circles us about 30 times, talking about everything from basketball to the latest movie. He usually had some corny saying that caused a wave of eye-rolling.

After getting a good stretch we took a few laps, mixed with some defensive slides on each baseline. At the conclusion, all the players gathered at the north basket just in front of the painted words "The PIT." We'd huddle up and, before breaking the huddle, all yell "PAC-10" to remind us of our goal—the PAC-10 championship.

Each practice we focused on the relationship between practice and the upcoming game. This year our practice had again carried over to our games, but the difference was consistency. A lot of players feel that practice is just the time you spend between games. As a team we knew we needed to get better each week. When we occasionally forgot, we got beat. By the end of the year practice became even more competitive. Interestingly enough, some of our best practices came in the last few weeks of the season.

SURPRISE

For some reason the UCLA game always had a different feel to it. Perhaps it was the history of the Bruin program, or maybe the fact that every year they are nationally ranked. Whatever it is, one thing stayed the same, beating UCLA always felt good. UCLA had been a mystery team for most of the year. One game the Bruins would look like the Lakers of old, scoring from everywhere on the floor, and other times they would look like junior high school team playing naked, awkward and unsure of what they were doing. They had a number of impressive wins, but just as many embarrassing losses. They had been the media's preseason pick to win the conference and even began the year ranked in the top five.

However at 6-3, UCLA was in second place and a game behind us. As usual, the game was significant for both teams. That week in practice we all anticipated a close contest that would become a possession game in the final minutes. "They will break; it might not come in the first half, but at some point they will break," Coach Kent told us throughout the week in practice and meetings. We knew that they were undisciplined and inconsistent.

With that in mind, our game plan was — what ever happened — to weather the storm. If UCLA came out shooting the lights out, then we needed to keep our composure and play solid defense until they leveled out. If they came out struggling, we needed to push them to their breaking point early, putting the game out of reach as quickly as possible.

From the moment we pulled up to Mac Court hours before tip-off, there was something different. The students were already lined up outside earlier than usual. In the locker room and training room there was a certain calm. Completely unaware we were balancing excitement and focus, our pre-game preparation felt pressure free. Coach talked repeatedly about playing our game, reminding us that to get into transition, we needed to get defensive stops.

The crowd was in rare form. They're allowed into the building an hour early. About six o' clock the doors open and the fans rush in to try and get the best spots in the student section.

When UCLA's players came onto the floor for the first time, the students started heckling and booing, talking about everything from mommas to haircuts. One group of guys sat right across from the bench every game. When I went up to the court to get up some shots, they started chanting my name, something I thought was a joke. So I tried to pretend that I wasn't listening. On my way down to the locker room, they flashed a sign that read, "Put Ben In." I smiled and made sure they knew I appreciated the support, but I wondered how much Coach Kent would.

From the tip both teams played at a blistering pace. We had waited all week to play the game and it showed. UCLA's players looked like they thought they were playing Oregon State first. We played one of our best halves of the season. Freddie was having a great game, but more importantly, so was every player who had stepped on to the floor. Big Chris was at his best, playing one of the best games of his career. All five starters where contributing offensively and defensively, and the bench was as solid as it had been all year, picking up where any starter left off.

The result was a 47-28 lead over the 13th-ranked Bruins through the first 20 minutes. The locker room at halftime was an interesting place to be since we were up 19 points, outplaying UCLA on both ends of the floor. What can a coach really say besides keep it up! We all knew they were out of the game but we still had another half of basketball. "I don't know if you realize how good we can be," Coach said in a philosophical tone.

In our 21st game of the season, we were just beginning to realize just how good we could be. Through an up-and-down preseason and then a solid first half of conference play, the things the coaches had been teaching us began to make sense.

In the second half we did more than keep it up; we started to make it embarrassing. About six minutes in the second half UCLA coach Steve Lavin decided he'd seen enough. He removed his starters and forced them to watch the embarrassment from the bench. The three best players on the UCLA team, Kapono, Gadzuric, and Barnes finished the game with a combined 14 points, shooting 6-of-25 from the floor.

Our team only got better in the second half. Chris continued to dominate the offensive and defensive boards, collecting a career-high 15 rebounds. Freddie continued to delight the crowd with spectacular plays, and finished with a game-high 28 points. Freddie had scored in double figures 15 straight games. When was the last time he had been in single digits? During our embarrassing loss at Portland.

By the end of the game we had set another record, Oregon's largest winning margin ever against UCLA, 29 points. And with a 91-62 win we were just four wins away from going undefeated at home. There were a number of elements to the story — Chris' big game, all five starters scoring in double figures, and the rock-solid play of Robert Johnson and the Lukes.

However, there was a much bigger story, Freddie Jones.

After three years of ridicule and questions about his work ethic and wasted potential, Freddie was quickly becoming more than just a spectacular dunker. He was becoming a consistent college superstar and, most importantly, our leader. In the past, article after article had talked about Freddie's disappointing performances. But now, the media was doing a 180, starting to write "feel good" stories about a player finally reaching his potential.

As I've said, it was always a great feeling to beat UCLA, but to beat them by just under 30 was even better. It was difficult not to feel a little prideful after the game, but as usual Coach Kent put everything into perspective, with the simple but true, "Don't get too high and don't get too low." We would be playing Saturday against USC for sole possession of first place. It was another chance to move a step closer to our goal.

HEAVYWEIGHTS

With a match up against the league-leading and 23rd ranked Trojans, both teams expected an intense hard-fought game. There would be no blowout like the UCLA game for us, or the OSU game for them.

Over the past four years the two teams had played only one game in which the winning margin was more than four points. In fact, our last home game with USC had been an overtime contest. With a great deal of senior leadership in their three best players, potential league MVP Sam Clancy, Brandon Granville and David Bluthenthal, it was apparent that the Mac Court crowd wouldn't be as effective as it is against younger players.

However, at home we were playing our best basketball, outscoring opponents by an average of over 20 points. Not only was our defensive intensity at another level, but our offense became even more explosive. Besides being a great place to play because of the consistent support, Mac Court seemed to always bring out the best in us. It's difficult to explain, but there is a certain energy that the crowd creates for a player. There have been times when the crowd became so intense that we felt unbeatable. It didn't matter what the other team did to try and stop it. I've even seen the officials caught up in the excitement of Mac Court at times.

With only a day to prepare we were forced to cram. USC ran a lot of things offensively and defensively, but this game would come down to who wanted it the most. There wasn't a lot that Coach Kent had to say; every player could sense the importance. It was finally starting to feel like college basketball should feel. This was why every player had come to Oregon, for a chance to play in front of a sell-out crowd with the conference lead at stake. With difficult games in the Bay Area and a trip to LA to finish up the year, a loss now could put us in a tough spot.

Coach Kent realized that there wasn't a lot that needed to be said, so he didn't say a lot. In a game like this it's important not to add any unneeded pressure. We went through the normal game preparation and headed down into the locker room for a few minutes of chalk talk and the team prayer.

We all stood in a circle, clasped hands and recited the Lord's Prayer. We had members of just about every religion in the room, but it didn't matter. It wasn't so much about the words in the prayer as it was about remembering that with all the importance the game held, there was still something more important. Whether it was God, family, or the inner spirit in each of us, we always took the time before and after the game to remember the more important things in life.

Just before going up onto the floor, we huddled as usual just inside the locker room to go through our pre-game chant. Just outside the door came the sound of, "Let's Go Ducks...Let's Go Ducks." The student section had lined up outside the doors of the locker room, making a tunnel that went up the stairs and all the way onto the floor. Forming the end of the line were the cheerleaders. After finishing our chant, we headed up to the floor through a sea of high fives and the occasional pat on the butt.

As we made our way onto the court, the band kicked in the school's fight song. After a few minutes of the routine lay-up drills, USC made its entrance to the deafening sound of boos and taunts from the student section. Within minutes we were ready to go. There was a nervous buzz in the air, and the look of two heavyweights circling each other at halfcourt, anticipating the tip.

The first few possessions each team was playing out its nervous energy. Both coaches were confidently strolling the sidelines, making sure the refs were earning their paychecks. Meanwhile the players themselves were getting a feel for the game, trying to control the momentum early. Each team would look like it was going to take control of the game, but that never happened. When one team got on a roll, the other team did just enough to stay close until its players could make their brief run.

Midway through the first half we started to slip a little. Freddie turned the ball over and USC guard Eric Craven sped down the floor for what looked like an easy basket and control of the momentum. Just before Craven could get off the ground to lay it up and in, Freddie raced down the court to join him. Freddie had made amazing plays all year, but as he took off the ground to contest the lay-up, everyone in the entire building held its collective breath sensing something was about to happen, but not knowing what. Craven now realized he would have to be more committed to the play if he wanted to get a basket or foul, so he decided to hold the ball a little longer and perhaps finish closer to the rim. As soon as he took off, Freddie made his move. As he glided through the air, he extended his arm and made a play on the ball. In slow motion he nearly palmed the ball in mid-air as it was leaving Craven's hand. Nobody knew what to expect when Freddie left the ground, but, as he came down with the ball in his hands, he had filled in the blank with one of the most exciting defensive plays of the year!

By the end of half it had become a classic college basketball game between two determined teams. We took a 43-40 lead into the locker room with the knowledge that there was a lot of basketball to still be played. Halftime was spent cleaning up some areas, and reinforcing our points of attack that had been successful. Luke Jackson had another great defensive effort in the first half on David Bluthenthal, in turn giving up a lot of his own opportunities, knowing that shutting down a part of their offense could be more effective.

The second half was played with the same intensity as the first. Neither team would back down. After a few minutes of trading baskets, we began to hit a dry spell from the outside, struggling to consistently score. Meanwhile, USC started to find a rhythm on offense as Sam Clancy was grabbing re-bounds and dominating the low post. At one point our shooting had gone so cold that we missed nine straight threes, and had fallen behind by six points with six minutes to go. With the score 63-57 in favor of USC, the game was starting to slip away. Then Freddie got open and drained a three that got the crowd back into the game. USC had done a good job in the second half of taking the crowd out of the game, a rare occurrence at Mac Court.

Up 63-60, USC started to rush things, resulting in a stolen pass that was thrown up to the floor to Rid. Running with him down the floor was a frustrated Granville, who looked like he was going to let Rid have the uncontested lay-up. Then out of nowhere he grabbed Rid and sent him to the floor. After such a bizarre play the refs had no choice but to call an intentional foul. Anything less would have sent the already angry crowd into a frenzy.

In a game where any error can change the game dramatically, or just turn into a missed opportunity, this particular play was the turning point. After going to the line for the two free throws, we were also given the ball on the sideline as a result of the intentional foul. After a difficult shooting performance, the free throws had been just the spark Rid needed. After the ball had come in and we had worked it around the floor, Rid got it and a little room. With Rid's quick release jump shot a little room was all he needed. With the flick of his wrist he let a three-pointer fly that had no choice but to go in. As the ball rattled in the crowd exploded, and we now led 65-63.

The crowd noise was deafening as USC took the ball down the floor on offense, everyone in the building expected them to panic. But, as though they were playing at home, the Trojans calmly worked the ball around the three-point line before tossing it into Clancy positioned in the low post. Without hesitation he took a dribble, faked to the middle, glided to the baseline and put up a short jumper. As the ball worked its way through the net, the noise drained out of the building and the game was tied.

Just like he'd done a hundred times in practice, Rid received the outlet pass, made his way down the left side, drove right at his defender, stopped at the three-point line and without thinking let it fly.

You can learn a lot about a player in the off-season, and in practice, but you really see what a player is made of when the game is on the line. As the ball left his hands I couldn't believe he was actually shooting the shot, the game was tied and each possession was priceless with so little time remaining.

However, you could tell that Rid knew exactly what he was doing. As the ball once again flew through the net, it became clear to everyone else.

The final minutes were at hand and the score was 68-65 in our favor. After a few seconds of relief, Sam Clancy got the ball again in the low post. This time he put up a tough shot that somehow found its way into the hoop. Each team was ineffective on the next two possessions before Clancy fouled Luke Jackson on a rebound. Jackson went to the line for what seemed like two automatic free throws.

Because we weren't in the double bonus, the trip to the line was a one-and-one instead of a two-shot foul. With a one-point lead and just over a minute left, Luke put up the first free throw. As it struck the front of the rim and bounced to USC, there was an overwhelming feeling of surprise and uncertainty, Luke had shown his surprise, too.

The Trojans systematically went down the floor, moving the ball around until Clancy got the ball, made a move and was fouled. Almost on cue, the crowd rose and made about as much noise as humanly possible.

Sitting on the bench on the other side of the court I had flashbacks of the incident two years earlier with USC's Granville at the free throw line. With the noise of the crowd I thought there was no way he was making more than one free throw, and that was being generous. Unfortunately, for everyone in the building cheering for Oregon, Clancy calmly made both, giving USC a one-point lead with less than a minute left.

Thirty-nine minutes of great basketball would come down to one possession. Without flinching we set up our halfcourt motion offense, not knowing really what our next move was. In late game situations Coach Kent rarely ran a set play unless it was to get a three. With three great scorers in Rid, Fred, and Jackson, we wanted to wait for a mismatch and take advantage.

After a few passes and screens, it happened, Clancy, a post player, was somehow switched onto Jackson, a guard. Immediately recognizing this, Jackson squared him up gave a few fakes and took the much slower defender to the basket. When he had gone as far as possible, Jackson gave one of his patented shot fakes to get Clancy into the air. Jackson did this at least 10 times a day in practice, and someone always jumped.

As Clancy left the ground Jackson waited for just the right time, leaning into Clancy's body and putting up an awkward shot. Clancy would have been fine, but, at the last second, he took a swing at the ball in an attempt to block it. The ball slipped out just before his hand came right down on Jackson's arm. As the referee's whistle sounded, the ball went up and over the rim, gently falling through the net.

The crowd erupted. The basket counted and Jackson was going to the foul line to give us a two-point lead that felt like 20.

"I wanted a chance to redeem myself," Luke said after the game, referring to his missed free throw a few possessions before. There were still 37 seconds to play, but that play had broken USC. Much like the Stanford game you could see it on their faces, even if they hadn't realized it. Luke made the free throw and, facing a 71-69 deficit, USC called a timeout to try and set up a play.

Although a clutch offensive performance had given us the lead, it would take a defensive stop to win the game. Fully expecting USC to go back to the well, Coach spent the timeout talking about trying to keep the ball out of Clancy's hands. He also discussed, whatever happened, not to give up a potential game-winning three.

When the timeout was over, both teams made their way onto the court unsure what the other had planned. USC in-bounded the ball and worked it around the perimeter, trying to pass it into a well-defended Clancy. Freddie got his hand on one pass that made its way out of bounds but not before a gasp from the nervous crowd. The ball came in again and USC's players started to panic, realizing there were only 10 seconds on the clock. Granville was desperately trying to find a good opportunity, and, after a few switches, found Bluthenthal at the top of the key.

Unlike the Portland game where a similar play requiring switches left a shooter wide open, this time there was a defender right there with a hand up as the shot left the hands of USC's best shooter.

From the angle on the bench it looked like the shot was going to bank in and give the Trojans an improbable one-point lead with only a few seconds left. After the shot made its way to the hoop, it careened off the rim and found a home in Freddie's hands, before being deflected out of bounds.

The Trojans scrambled to steal the inbounds pass, but were forced to foul James Davis. With just over a second left, James confidently made both free throws, giving us a 73-69 lead. After someone from USC threw up a meaningless prayer from halfcourt, the game was over and somehow we had found a way to win.

"Good ball clubs find a way to win" Jackson simply but profoundly put it after the game. The win felt great. We were in sole possession of first place and still undefeated at home.

As a team we were starting to figure it out. USC was, without question, the best team we had played to date. We hadn't played exceptionally well and still came away with the victory. After congratulating us, Coach gave us the next two days off, but reminded us not to let our celebration last much longer than the night, knowing full well that the Bay Area held an even greater challenge.

Dealing with the media afterwards was an exhibition of saying all the right things. Even after a huge win Rid easily described our mindset, "We've got a lot to prove; we're going to feel good about ourselves tonight. But it's way too early to celebrate. We've still got a lot to prove on the road."

Downplaying the situation even more, Freddie reminded the media of our most important goal; "Right now it doesn't mean that much where we are in the standings. We want to be in first place when it ends."

After the game I had to wonder what the USC locker room was like game. I could easily picture the USC players sitting in the other side of Mac Court wondering what had just happened. In a game in which there had been 14 lead changes and the score had been tied 13 times, they seemed to have been in control down the stretch, only to have the game quickly change directions, leaving them with a four-point loss.

To my surprise the next day, my questions were answered. USC had not been as graceful as I had imagined. They seemed to feel that we stole the victory from them, and hinted that although we had won, we still weren't the best team in the conference. Setting the stage early for a potential title-deciding game in LA, Clancy said this on his way out of the locker room, "We still get to play them at home; let's not forget that!"

While eating breakfast the next morning I couldn't help but get a kick out of his comment. Little did he know that we looked forward to that game just as much as he did!

CHAPTER 7
The Greatest Game Never Televised

"Experience is one thing you can't get for nothing." — *Oscar Wilde*

By the time we were finishing weights on Monday, our second day off after one of the biggest weekends at Mac Court in years, the Associated Press Top 25 poll came out. We had entered the week unranked, and, after the big weekend were ranked No. 13 in the country. It is always exciting to be ranked in the top 25, but No.13 in the country had a nice ring to it; it meant we were that close to getting into the top 10.

More important than the ranking was the fact that we were in first place, having beaten all the five contending teams. For the first time in school history we had five victories over ranked teams, an impressive record for any school. With a month to play, we were in the in the driver's seat, 17-5, with a 9-2 record in the conference.

Before we headed down to the Bay Area it was important that we not pay attention to the repeated talk of being a poor road team. "We haven't been blown out by anyone," Coach said in reference to the number of close losses we had on the road. In our five losses, our average margin of defeat was five points. In fact we hadn't lost a game by more than seven points the entire season. We had a chance in the final minutes to win every game.

"You have to play twice as good on the road," Coach Kent told us as we started the week. We had grown accustomed to the friendly confines of Mac

Court, and oftentimes found it easy to get away with poor shooting or a few defensive lapses. However, it was a much different story on the road. Stanford and Cal would be the toughest road games thus far. If we came home with two losses, we would certainly be between a rock and a hard spot.

Stanford desperately needed a win. With four losses in the conference, the Cardinal was in danger of completely slipping out of contention, and was even in danger of missing the NCAA tournament.

After two days off and a few days of practice, we headed to the Bay Area, had dinner, and checked into our hotel. In terms of hotels, the Stanford trip has the nicest, the Stanford Park Hotel. Supposedly it's where President Clinton used to stay when he visited his daughter Chelsea while she attended Stanford.

Before we pulled up to the hotel, Freddie came back and reminded Anthony and I of the cookies and milk that were regularly placed in the lobby around 9:30. The new guys had no idea so it was crucial that we get off the bus and get to them before the guys with the unlimited appetites did.

PAPER, ROCK, SCISSORS

Every road trip when we check into the hotel, we get our room assignments from the front desk as Hud hands out the keys with the name of the roommate. About halfway through the season everyone tries to switch the assignment. Rid and I were usually together and Anthony was usually with Rob. Anthony and I were the clean freaks on the team, so we'd always try and room together. I would either give Rob my key, or Anthony would give Rid his. By the time we got to Stanford, this had become somewhat of a tradition. A couple of other guys did the same thing; Freddie roomed with James Davis every trip. After awhile, the roommate thing had become a superstition with some of the guys.

Luke gliding effortlessly through the air.

The only problem in the deal was that sometimes the rooms weren't all in the same area. Someone could wind up five minutes away from where we meet or even from his closest teammate. To handle this Rid and I decided to play Paper, Rock, Scissors to decide who got the better room. On this trip I had the farthest room, so it was in my best interest to win. The rules were simple, best out of three, and no complaining. After a 1-1 tie, I went with Rock, and Rid went with Paper, sending me to the farthest room.

Somehow Anthony and I got the room that was the furthest from anything in the hotel, including the majority of the places where we met and ate. When we came to the door, the room was already open and some kind of air purifier that sounded like highway traffic was running. Anthony and I looked at each other, wondering if we had stumbled into the wrong room. Exhausted from our long walk from the elevator, we threw our bags onto the bed. After a few minutes the smell of cigarette smoke in the room became unbearable, and we quickly realized the purpose of the air purifier, we had originally thought was a room upgrade.

After taking a shower, I jokingly put on the complimentary robe, and walked into the bedroom to make a phone call. The hotel had a number of comfortable features including, a CD player, big rooms, cordless phones, and my favorite, the fancy robes.

I picked up the cordless phone to make a call. Just then a maintenance guy walked into the room.

Here I was in a robe that was a little too small, on a cordless phone and pacing around the room. I was not only embarrassed, but also really starting to wonder if we had the wrong room. The worker didn't speak any English, so I had no idea what was going on, Luckily Anthony spoke Spanish. After a few minutes of conversation, the guy picked up the air purifier and walked out of the room.

Anthony informed me that the room had been cleaned and the worker was just there to pick up the purifier. Unfortunately, the smell of smoke was still present so we asked to switch rooms. After about a half-hour we got a new room and went to bed.

GAME DAY

Of all the places to play in the conference, Stanford is probably the most interesting. Whether it's the floor, the student section, the cheerleaders, or the adult fans, one thing is for sure, there is no other place like it. The floor is like a giant wood trampoline. It is a suspended floor that bounces about six inches in some places.

My first year I saw a piece on the news that showed a camera on one end of the floor while someone was playing on the other end. The camera almost 90 feet away from the action was bouncing up and down. The first time anybody steps onto the floor, you feel like you've just stepped onto a fishing boat. It takes a minute to get a feel for it, but within a few minutes you feel like you can touch the top of the backboard.

After every practice or shoot-around, there are always a few guys who try to do an array of dunks. This usually included me. I am the type of jumper who likes to jump off one foot. I have to be pretty loose to dunk off two feet, but at Stanford such a move comes surprisingly easy. I usually spend the time after practice trying to do different dunks, usually in front of some of the guys waiting for me to get hung or Coach Kent to say, "Ben, that's enough," which usually came first.

Another interesting element is the student section. Those students always have something intelligent to yell and have an array of cheers. My favorite is probably when a player for the opposing team fouls out. Once the foul is called, and the player heads for the bench, the fans take over the building. They meet each footstep with a chant of, "left…right…left…right." This is done until the player reaches the bench. Once he gets there, they finish with "Sit Down!"

Now this would be mildly amusing if a few hundred people did it, but the entire student section and a number of other fans take part in this perfectly executed tradition. Two of the three years I have played down there, Chris has fouled out, and it seemed like the crowd was usually in rare form when he made the trip to the bench.

Chris would have a little fun with this too. He would run and then walk and the crowd would speed up and slow down. He even tried stopping just before he got to the bench, but the crowd knew he had to sit down, patiently waited and was particularly loud when they finally said, "Sit Down." Even in the most serious of games this brought a smile from our bench, this occurrence was so amusing that sometimes I hoped for someone to foul out if it didn't have an effect on the game.

After the shoot-around, we headed back to the hotel, relaxed for a few hours then came back to the gym, Maples Pavilion. Maples only holds about 7,500, but it can get just as loud as a 14,000-seat arena. The game was a sellout, and we knew it would be a loud evening. Before we headed onto the floor, Coach Kent motioned to our team manager Greg Lawrence to read a flier he nervously held in his hands.

Apparently those in the student section receive at newsletter called something like the 6th Man. It comes complete with a joke or piece of information about each player that is to be used as a heckling tool before, during, and after each game.

Greg stood in the back of the room and read the newsletter. It covered everything from cuss words in Danish to yell at Chris Christofferson, who's from Denmark; to a joke about Brian Helquist's final Internet art project that they somehow tracked down. It also had a few jokes about the Lukes' hairdos being related to the characters in the movie and book Lord of the Rings. The pressure before the game had begun to be noticeable, and this was exactly what we needed. After a few minutes of laughter we felt loose and headed to the floor.

For some strange reason, someone had decided our game would not be televised. Apparently the game between ninth place Oregon State and fourth place Cal looked like it had all the makings of a good basketball game. Of course it was a laugher, but that wasn't the only problem. Because the PAC-10 sold its rights to Fox Sports, no other games can be broadcast without permission. KEZI, a local Oregon station which broadcasts a number of games during the year, had petitioned to do the game but permission had been denied.

So the only cameras that would film the game were the few news cameras on the baselines. They were only there to get a few highlights for the evening news. Other than that the lone school camera in the cheap seats so far away that making out numbers on film took a few rewinds of the recorded action.

Just before the tip you could see desperation on the faces of the Stanford players, and you could sense the desire to win we had shown all through warm-ups and to start the game. The game got off to a quick start; Stanford not only had a look of desperation, but was playing the same way. Jacobsen had caught fire again, and Curtis Borchardt seemed ready to have another big game. Jacobsen had dropped 32 points on us in Eugene and seemed determined to do the same thing at home. The first half featured a number of great plays, from fancy passes to long-range shooting. After we had been down by five points and closing in on the halfway point, Freddie and Luke managed to hit back-to-back threes that sparked us back to life and sent us into the locker room tied 34-34.

It had been a while since we had been in a game at Stanford through 20 minutes of play. Usually that's about the time the Cardinal had started to pull away. However, a lot of things were different this year, and for the first time in a Stanford locker room we sat feeling confident that we were in great position to get our first win since the 1980's. Coach Kent reassured us that the game was ours for the taking. We just needed to continue to play solid and pick up the defense on the same two guys who had hurt us in Eugene.

Both teams jockeyed for position to start the second half. We built a four-point lead, and it felt like we might be the one's pulling away. Then Freddie was whistled for an offensive foul that looked a lot more like a blocking foul on Stanford than anything else. The momentum quickly changed hands and Stanford reeled off six straight points, taking a 47-45 lead.

For the next 10 minutes the game went back and forth, featuring more spectacular plays from both teams.

After getting down a few, we made a run of our own that featured one of the most spectacular Freddie Jones dunks. Stanford turned the ball over and Freddie received it around the three-point line, took one dribble and took off outside the lane. Going right over the defender while cocking the ball behind his head with one hand, he then sent the ball through the hoop with Shaq-like force. He was so high his defender couldn't even foul him. This even surprised the crowd and forced them to catch themselves before cheering for such a spectacular play by the opposing team. Our bench however, erupted, and had to be warned by an official to sit down.

THE GUY BEHIND THE BENCH

Maples Pavilion is more like a giant high school gym than a college basketball arena. The majority of the seating is wood bleachers, and the hoops are connected to the ceiling as opposed to the now common freestanding portable hoops. The home crowd sits about four feet from the visitors' bench, a little too close for comfort for the teams, but no doubt a great seat for any fan. As the game was coming down the stretch, there was a guy behind the bench who would get on his cell phone and pretend like he was relaying our discussions during each timeout.

As the game got closer and closer he became even more animated, and was even able to inspire another fan to take part. The guy was only four feet away so it felt like he was right there in our huddle. I think for the first couple of timeouts we thought he really might be on the phone discussing the plays and strategies we were covering. The "guy behind the bench" as we referred to him, was acting out a very believable performance. After awhile Josh, our graduate manager, would go behind the bench during timeouts and block the guy's view with a clipboard. This seemed to only encourage more dramatic expressions from the guy.

Just like the student section at Stanford, the regular fans are also a little different. I still laugh when I think about my first experience at Maples Pavilion. During the first timeout of the game I was in the huddle facing the crowd, and noticed about three fans behind the bench reading books. I had never seen anything like that, and assumed that it was just a one-time deal. However, over the next two years I saw the same thing from more than just a few fans. I knew that Stanford is known as an elite academic school, but I couldn't help but laugh at the fact that they were reading books during timeouts.

With about two minutes to play the game was tied at 71 a-piece. In all my years of watching and playing basketball, I had never been as nervous as I was then. It had turned into one of those games that you talk about 25 years later. I wanted to win so badly, but both teams had played so well that, as a fan of the game, you hoped it wouldn't end. Freddie had played one of his best games I had seen in the three years I'd played with him. He finished the game with 36 points on 12-of-19 shooting, 10 rebounds, three assists and three steals.

Luke Jackson and Rid had solid games, picking up 17 and 18 points apiece, including six assists for Rid and seven boards for Jackson. To help the cause Robert Johnson, who is usually the model of consistency, stepped up his game even more for his return to Northern California, notching 10 points and 13 boards. Stanford was not without the spectacular either. Jacobsen was on his way to an outstanding 41 points, while Borchardt was doing the rest with 24 points and 15 rebounds.

The last minute felt like 10. Stanford was running out of time, while, for us the clock couldn't move quickly enough. With 45 seconds left we had a 76-75 lead. Then Jacobsen missed and Freddie went to the line for a pair of free throws. I could hardly watch, but Freddie coolly knocked down both, giving us a three-point lead and some breathing room with 14 seconds left. Coach called a timeout. With a three-point lead we wanted to give up anything but a three. Part of our plan was to keep the ball out of the hands of one of the best shooters in college basketball, Casey Jacobsen. We discussed the idea of fouling and giving up two free throws and still getting the ball back with the lead, but this didn't seem like a good idea for the time and situation.

When the ball came in, it was obvious they were going to have Jacobsen shoot the last shot. However, when the Cardinal got the ball to Jacobsen, he was well covered and would have only been throwing up an ill-advised prayer. So to just about everyone's surprise, he gave the ball to one of the worst shooters on his team, Tony Giovacchini. Finding himself well behind the three-point line with time running out he set up and fired the shot. As I watched the shot, I thought, "thank goodness he's shooting it, and not anybody else."

Fully expecting the ball to fire off the top of the backboard, I was sick when it rattled in. The game was tied with four seconds left. Jackson was able to get a last-second shot off that just about went in but it bounced away as time expired. The building felt like it was going to come down. I couldn't tell if it was the buzz of surprise, or celebration. Giovacchini, the most unlikely of heroes had tied the game and stolen back the momentum, his stats, 32 minutes, 1-for-3 from the field.

Getting the momentum back after a play like that is very difficult. We had one of our biggest wins of the season in the bag, and somehow we were going to overtime. In the huddle we looked a little like a dazed fighter in the 12th round. We had fought our hearts out; we thought we had our opponent knocked out and then got a left hook from just outside the three-point line. After a few minutes in our corner, we headed back out to finish the fight. I wasn't sure what was going to happen. We were only a few fouls away from losing Chris, Brian, and most importantly, Freddie.

In a game that had been so exciting, there was no way the overtime was going to be uneventful. After trading baskets, Stanford had an 82-81 lead when Giovacchini got another wide-open look. Gathering himself, he confidently shot it up. As my eyes followed the ball. I was expecting the worst, but when the ball missed badly, it only made his lone basket of the game seem more unbelievable.

After the miss we took the ball down the floor and took the lead with a Ridnour bucket. That shot was the last time we led, Stanford was starting to get its second wind, and game was getting away from us. Within the next few minutes we found ourselves without the services of Chris, Brian and finally Freddie on an even more questionable call than the one in the first half. After making a final push by Rid, the game was over and Stanford had won, 90-87.

To our surprise the fans rushed the floor in celebration. At the time we didn't think much of it. After all, it had been a great game and they had reason to be excited. However, later after thinking about it, it seemed to tell more about our program than it did about the game. Fans rushing the floor is something that is usually reserved for upsets of smaller programs over a powerhouse.

A win at Mac Court over Stanford is something that deserves swarming the floor because the Cardinal have dominated the conference for years and we have been fighting to get into the top half on a consistent basis. But the fans at Stanford rushing the floor after a victory over Oregon... Perhaps we were getting closer to becoming one of those types of teams after all.

It was one of the greatest college basketball games I had ever seen. It had featured amazing performances by a number of players on both teams. The crowd was into the game from tip off until well after the final buzzer had sounded. Throughout the course of the game I kept talking to anybody that would listen saying, "How can this game not be televised?" By the end of the game, even after a heart-breaking loss, I felt confident that the overtime battle could have been, the greatest game never televised!

We had somehow reached our breaking point first. We were the better team; we even played what felt like the better game, but we were leaving with a loss and a wasted opportunity to distance ourselves from five other teams. The locker room was full of shocked looks, and hung heads. It's hard to describe the feelings after a tough loss; the roller coaster seemed like it had no end. After the game Anthony and I talked about how it seemed like every time we got in a good position, we lost. It was something that had started from the beginning of the season and was continuing its vicious cycles even late in the year.

Coach Kent was positive after the game. He had sensed the fragility of our team and realized that our next game was now more important than dwelling on a disappointing loss. Arizona was now tied with us for the league lead, so a possible loss two days later at Cal would not only bump us from the top, but could easily throw us back to sixth place where we would be near the bottom looking up.

CAL: CLOSE BUT NO CIGAR!

After a disappointing loss at Stanford, the next day was about two things, rest and energy. An overtime loss had taken a toll physically and mentally. Although we didn't believe the talk about being a poor road team, at 3-6 on the road it was hard to overlook. Friday, the day after the loss and the day before the national televised match-up with Cal, was spent getting our energy back and resting.

The drive from Stanford to Cal was about an hour. We woke up, had breakfast and headed to Berkley. The bus was silent for most of the drive. The coaches had thrown some game film of the Oregon State-Cal game from the night before onto the bus TV's to begin our preparation. As usual we drove straight to the arena to practice before checking in at the next hotel.

Practice was spent getting up shots and walking through Cal's plays. Before we took the floor Coach made sure that we knew practice was going to be short but he wanted us to be sharp. When we stepped onto the floor everyone looked tired and a step slow. After some standard shooting drills, we walked through their plays. Although everyone felt like sleeping, the walk-through was surprisingly sharp and intense.

After about an hour Coach was satisfied and gave us a few minutes to shoot while he talked to Jay Bilas, who was announcing the game for ABC the next day. Bilas also co-hosts ESPN's College Hoops Tonight, and had looked forward to seeing an upstart Oregon team that he later said had all the keys to get to the Final Four.

The Claremont Hotel where we stay when we play Cal is a huge building that sits up on the hills of Berkley overlooking the entire Bay Area. It is an older hotel that reminds me of the Great Gatsby days. Each room is very different. Usually one guy got a really big room, and another ended up with a room the size of a deluxe janitor's closet. After winning the battle of Paper,

Rock Scissors, Anthony and I ended up with a great room close to the elevator. This became even more valuable than at Stanford; the hotel was huge and the last place you wanted to be was at the end of one of the massive halls.

Somehow Jay tricked me into finding out just how long the halls could be. He told me to come down to his room for a minute, so I headed down there and, after about five minutes, wondered if I had the room number mixed up.

Finally after about a 10-minute walk I arrived at his door, walked in and said, "What do you need?" He simply replied, "Oh, nothing."

Quickly realizing what was going on, I admitted he had got me, looked out his window that over looked the service entrance, laughed and said, "you deserve it" as I walked out with a smile on my face and a long walk ahead. On the way back I passed Chris' room, stopped in and told him that Jay's room was huge and he should go check it out. Chris's reply was, "nice try; he already got me."

After a few hours of relaxing, we met in the lobby, we hopped onto the bus and went to dinner. When we go to dinner, Coach Kent usually doesn't go unless we eat on our way from the airport to the hotel. Other than that, the team, Hud, Josh, Clay, and Greg are the only ones who go to dinner although occasionally Jerry Allen will join us. This is the time that we have the majority of the fun. Hud is always good about letting us pick the restaurant, and we usually even catch a movie if it starts early enough.

On the bus the first thing that happens is you hear Freddie's voice from the back of the bus telling the driver to turn the radio on. This became a regular occurrence, the station of choice—anything with Rap or R&B. Even when all the coaches were on the bus the radio was played, usually as loud as possible. I highly doubt that any other coaches let the their players not only listen to the radio, but pick the station and the volume. There were even a few times on the way to games that we listened to the radio.

After dinner and a movie at a restored theater in downtown Oakland, we arrived back at the hotel to meet in one of its many ballrooms. Assuming we were going to have another walk-through, we all waited as the coaches trickled in. In the front of the room was a small table with a tablecloth that draped to the floor. Because it was right in front of where everyone was sitting and you had to pass it to sit down, I decided to hide underneath. The idea was that as soon as someone walked by I would grab his leg and scare the crap out of him.

As the players sat around, I poked my head out and told them to give a signal when someone was coming. All the players were already there so we were waiting for a coach to walk by. They had told us that because we had eaten earlier and we were going to bed earlier than usual because of an afternoon start the next day, they would order a few pizzas to eat after the meeting.

I could tell that someone had walked in because the room went quiet and I could hear a few guys holding in their laughter. I never heard the signal, but knew somebody was standing right next to the table. So as soon as I saw a shoe, I reached out, grabbed the leg and yelled, "AHHHHH."

Everyone busted up laughing and I thought for sure that I had scared Hud or Josh. When I slid out from the confines of the table I quickly realized why no signal had been given. The pizza deliveryman stood there with a stunned look on his face, not sure what was going on. After a few minutes he got his money and quickly exited the room.

Coach Kent had now entered the room, but we were still waiting for Coach Graham. The plan was to tell him to grab a slice of pizza from the table that I was once again hiding under. After a few minutes of waiting, the signal was given, I heard Coach Kent tell him to grab some pizza.

For a minute I hesitated, worrying that he might have a heart attack or throw out his already injured back. However, when he got so close to the table that his shoes were creeping in, I raised both arms, reached out and with even more excitement in my voice screamed, "AAAHHHH." After a quick jolt, he was now trying to get away from my grip and made a similar, "AHHHH" while almost knocking the boxes of pizza off the table. Everyone broke into laughter, he still had no idea what was happening until I crawled out from under the table and checked to make sure he wasn't mad or bent over nursing his back.

After a few minutes of laughter, Coach stood up and began discussing the importance of the game. Immediately everyone's attention was back on the task at hand. We had a fun evening, and we now realized that it was time to start thinking about tomorrow. I always thought that part of our success was the ability to focus and relax at the right times. Some teams struggle distinguishing between the two. We however, were able to go from laughing hysterically to discussing players' tendencies. Coach Kent understood this and regularly used it to guide us from game to game.

Coach felt that rest was more important than walking through their plays again. This was a good thing for us, so, without asking any questions, we teamed it up and headed off to our rooms.

For some reason breakfast on game day is always quiet; there will be an occasional laugh, but, for the most part things are silent. After a tough loss, the day of the game feels even slower than usual; you usually sit around the hotel and watch the other games as you wait to depart to the arena.

Haas Pavilion is a newly remodeled arena that holds right around 12,000 fans. Similar to Mac Court, the fans feel like they are close enough to the court to reach out and grab you. The band is seated right next to the visitors' bench. In fact, its members are so close that you really feel like reaching out and grabbing someone. They were so close that by halftime I had a headache from their excessive play. Along with tormenting the visitors with their instruments, there are always a few guys in the band who make it their sole purpose at the game to constantly be yelling something.

Warm-ups always seem to be an exercise in patience. Fans often cross the line. As a heckler at games myself, I always fight the urge to yell something back. On a couple of trips I was told by Coach Kent not to say anything to the crowd, but often I mumbled something to the occasional fan that crossed the line.

During this game there happened to be this little girl, probably about 10 years old, who was sitting with her mom and dad. During a timeout I noticed her making faces at me, I thought it was a cute gesture by a little girl at first but right in front of her parents she started yelling, "you're ugly!" I almost couldn't believe my ears until she blurted out, "yeah, you" even louder. I thought for sure her parents would put an end to it. I know my parents still wouldn't let me yell anything like that to another person.

Next thing I know her parents are encouraging her. I thought for sure they must have all been on crazy pills. Like a little kid myself, I couldn't refuse the opportunity to respond. I began to mouth similar childish responses like, "look in the mirror" and a few Mickey Mouse references to her unusually big ears. The whole time I refrained from anything out of line to make sure that a security guard didn't have to haul me off in the middle of the game for yelling at a 10-year-old.

When the game started, all but a hand full of the 12,000 were in their seats, the members of the student section were on their feet, and once again it felt like the start of another great college basketball game. The biggest concern going into the game was our energy after a draining loss, it was crucial that we didn't come out, as Coach Kent often said, and "lay an egg."

Within the first two minutes we had erased those concerns. Freddie led the charge, doing just about everything, scoring, rebounding, and dishing out assists to wide-open shooters. With about 2 ½ minutes left in the first half we had built a 19-point lead and Cal was the team without energy. Since we had a 45-26 lead the game looked like it was going to be over before the half. But then Cal finished with a blurring 11-3 run that did more than cut the lead to 48-35. The crowd, who had been silently watching our offensive clinic, was waiting for any chance to cheer for the home team Bears, and the run was just what it needed.

In the locker room we were determined to get refocused. We had played a great 17 ½ minutes and still had a 13-point lead. We knew full well that Cal and its fans would start the second half with more energy than they did in the first. With 20 minutes to play, the most important thing was getting out of there with the win, if it was by 20 or 1 it didn't matter. Up to that point in the season we hadn't panicked once at the half, and this hardly seemed like the time or the place.

The effects of the first half still lingered when the second began. We had given Cal just enough room to breathe. As funny as it sounds, sometimes teams aren't sure they can really beat another team, and when they experience a little success they begin to realize they're not out of the game as far as they think. This is exactly what had happened to us; through the first 17 minutes you could tell that Cal's players thought they were going to get beat by 30. It only took a few bad decisions on our part and a few shots to fall for them before they suddenly realized that they were back in the game.

The pace of the first 10 minutes was in their favor. They were slowly getting closer until a 3-three pointer had given the Bears a 58-56 lead. We had been playing not to lose, and, when the lead turned into a deficit, we were once again playing to win. Unfortunately, we had waited too long so we found ourselves right in the middle of another battle. Cal's Amit Tamir, a 6-foot-10 freshman from Jerusalem, had found his game late in the first half, and picked up right where he had left off in the second. Much like Jacobsen two nights before, he was scoring from everywhere including the outside.

The game had gone back and forth, but with a few minutes to play we still managed to hold an 80-75 lead. A couple of defensive stops and the game would be over. However, Tamir was far from letting the game be over. The very next possession he came down and fired a three in from the top of the key, and, after a stop on the other end, was fouled and put in two free throws to tie the game. Without flinching we took the ball down and went to Jackson, who delivered a tough basket. Nearing the final minute, I started to feel like we just might escape with the victory. Then Tamir tied the game again, this time with an inside basket.

Unable to score on our next possession, we were forced to defend a potential game-winning shot by Cal at the other end. Patiently working the ball around, Cal finally ran out of shot clock and point guard Shantay Legans was forced to put up a jump shot that never had a chance. Then as Freddie often did, he spectacularly snatched the ball out of the air, and was on his way down the floor racing against the regulation clock and the Cal defense.

With a matter of seconds left, Freddie found himself inside the three-point line with Legans, who had barely managed to get in front as Freddie left the ground to lay the ball up. Fearing the offensive foul that had forced him out of the Stanford game, Freddie shifted mid-air, sliding his body around Legans who was trying to fake the charge. As the clock neared zeroes, Freddie gently finger-rolled the ball up and over the rim. As the entire bench jumped up, expecting the shot to fall, it slid off the side and Cal got it before the horn sounded.

For the second time in three days, we were headed to overtime. To start the overtime Tamir was once again relentless. This time we matched every shot and, as the overtime was coming to an end, we held an uncomfortable 88-86 lead. Just like the Bears had done the whole second half, they went down to the other end and answered, this time with what felt like a backbreaking three with under a minute left. Close games were no stranger to our team, so, without missing a beat, we set up an isolation play for Freddie that drew a foul with only 23 seconds left.

Freddie was only able to convert on 1-of-2 free throws, tying the game at 89-89. With time running out and the game tied, Cal appeared content to let the game go to the second overtime. As the Bears cautiously passed the ball around, we somehow forced a turnover, but were unable to convert any last-second heroics.

Cal dominated the second overtime; Tamir fired in another three, finishing the game with a monster 39-point game that felt like 50! Legans also connected and before we knew it the score was 97-89 for Cal. After getting it close a few times, we had finally broken, and Cal escaped with a 107-103 double overtime win.

The locker room had a much different tone than it had after the Stanford game just two days earlier. We had been swept and were now in a five-way tie for second place. It felt like a bad dream; we had gone into the weekend in first place, and were leaving the Bay Area with two heart-breaking losses. Our chance at a championship seemed to have disappeared with each lead we lost in the last few minutes.

When Coach Kent entered the locker room, he was struggling to put an angle on the game. For someone that could spin the worst loss into a positive, he also felt the uncertainty that hovered in the locker room. "There's one reason we lost this game," he said. After scoring 103 points it didn't take a basketball analyst to tell it wasn't our offense. "Defense," he said with a sigh. We all knew it, in the two games we had played one guy scored 41, and another scored 39. The worst part was that most of their points came at critical times.

We were starting to feel like Dr. Jekyll and Mr. Hyde. At home our offense and defense seemed to be played on another level, yet on the road, we only seemed to pack our offense! Freddie had given us another brilliant performance with 23 points, seven rebounds, and six assists. Luke Jackson added to the cause with a career-high 29 points, shooting 10-of-14 from the field while picking up a solid four boards and five assists. Yet somehow we had lost, giving up ground we had worked so hard to gain.

After the game Freddie took the loss especially hard. He felt that he should have won the game with the lay-up in the final seconds and again with a missed free throw at the end of the first overtime. As a team we knew better. Freddie had played two great games, and the real reason for the loss was not a foul shot or missed lay-up, but our defense (or lack of it!). Reality set in quickly after the game. If we were going to have a real chance at a champion-ship we would have to win on the road, and in order to win we needed defense!

We had played two great games, two championship-type games, but we were on our way back to Eugene with nothing but two losses to show for our efforts. We had come so close. It was difficult not to think about what would have happened if we had won both games. Instead we took the traffic-filled drive over the Bay Bridge to the airport, arriving back in Eugene just before midnight.

The best Fans in College Basketball...The "PIT CREW."

CHAPTER 8
The wrong place at the wrong time!

*"Losing is a lens through which you can
see yourself more clearly" — Phil Jackson*

After the losses in the Bay Area it was a strange time for our team. We had
lost some tough games already that year, but these hurt a lot more. With our
next game a week away, we were given a few days off; everyone was emotion-
ally and physically exhausted. There are a number of defining moments in life,
and a basketball season is no different. It would have been easy to feel like we
already accomplished a great deal, and a trip to the NCAA tournament would
be enough to represent that, but our other option was to win our last five
games, three at home and the final two in LA.

So what does a team do in that position? Well, Coach Kent had finally
begun to rub off on us and we decided to spin one of the lower points of the
season to our advantage.

"I was disappointed, I knew we let it slide, but you could feel us getting
better. I realized a few days after that those games only helped us get closer to
where we wanted to be" Ridnour later reflected. " By losing it only made us
hungrier!"

After a few days off, in practice you could see exactly what Rid was
referring to. Just as so much of the off-season had helped shape our team,
once the hurting wore off our team felt even stronger. And, as usual, Coach

Kent made sure that there were no questions about where this team was headed. "Our goal is to win our last three games at home, sending the seniors out with a wonderful celebration," he said to start the weekly team meeting off.

So without thinking so much about wining the PAC-10 championship, our goal was to finish what we had started just over three months ago, going undefeated at home. At that point, we were the only team in the conference yet to lose at home. And the last team to actually go 16-0 at home was in 1938. If we got the three-game sweep we would certainly be contributing to even more history, becoming one of only three other teams in school history to ever go undefeated at home.

Much like the first installment of the Civil War, Oregon State was again desperate for a win in order to stay in the three-team race for the final spot in the PAC-10 tournament. Our team, on the other hand, had a bad taste in its mouth that made for a lively week of practice. After the tough week we took a good look at ourselves, and realized like so many other times in the season that we weren't quite there yet, and we needed to make some adjustments if we wanted to get there.

As usual Coach Litz went back to work on the basics. At this point in the season you'd think he would have started to get frustrated with 15 guys who thought they knew it all. However, with a mad scientist's grin, he went back to work, making sure that we were reminded of why we had been successful. Our defense on the road was not poor because of a lack of hard work or effort, but instead because we were mentally breaking down by failing to do the little things. As Litz often said, "The little things add up to big things."

In the days leading up to the game, we were saying all the right things and so were the guys at OSU. Each team talked about what the other team did well, very rarely talking about what they did poorly. OSU was catching us at a bad time, coming off two losses in a row. On the other hand, we saw this game as a chance to take our frustration out.

Once again the game was on a Saturday because it was our only conference game of the week. It had been a long wait, but it was finally over. The game was sold out and the fans always enjoyed a chance to cheer against the Beavers. In the locker room before the game Litz plugged defense once again with his rivalry speech that he'd used in the first Civil War game.

It felt good to be home again, and when the game began our play reflected those same feelings. We jumped out to an early 18-4 lead, and looked to finish them off when they started to chip away at the lead, fighting back to get within 28-25. At that point we appeared to receive a slap in the face that only fired us up even more.

What followed was one of the most amazing runs I had ever seen as we closed the half with a 17-2 run and took a 48-27 lead into the locker room. Halftime felt like it lasted forever. Our defense was coming back around and our offense couldn't miss, we couldn't wait to get back up on the floor for the second half.

Without missing a beat, we picked up right where we left off. With about 13 minutes left we had gone on a 41-11 run that featured a great defense mixed perfectly with a potent offense. The run finally ended with the 69-36 lead and the game well out of hand. We had built a 37-point lead before calling the dogs off, finishing the game off with a 91-62 win. Freddie, Jackson and Rid once again led the charge, scoring 62 of the 91 points. Robert, Chris and the rest of the bench contributed at all the right times.

Oregon State's head coach Ritchie Mckay summed up the intangibles we had acquired throughout the past 10 months, and one of the keys to winning the game "They could care less who scores; Ernie's team has no selfishness."

We had played one of our best defensive games of the year, applying a smothering full court press and intense defense on each possession. In the locker room after the game, we felt like a frustrated fighter who had just taken everything out on a punching bag. As we plopped down in our seats, everyone looked around, breathing a sigh of relief and flashing a smile. It felt good, similar to when you have a bad day, come home and vent your frustration by telling the day's stories, finishing and saying out loud, "that feels a lot better." Oregon State had simply stumbled into the wrong place at the wrong time.

Things certainly felt better. After feeling like we had taken the control out of our hands with two crucial losses, things had once again gone our way. First-place Arizona had lost to UCLA on Thursday and again on Saturday to USC, and Cal, which was tied for second, was also tripped up by the Huskies of Washington. Once again we found ourselves in first place and back in control of our destiny. Four wins would secure us at least a piece of the conference title, and perhaps sole possession with the top six teams all facing each other in the final weekend of the regular season.

Just after the game the managers brought the game ball down to the locker room to be kept in a separate place. Each year there is a ball that is deemed the game ball. This ball, once worn in, is hardly practiced with and usually kept separate from the other balls. You couldn't play with just any ball. Usually the game ball had the perfect feel to it. Whether it was just enough air, or had been worn in just right, the game ball was always better than the others on the rack. Written just below the Spalding insignia were 14 X's, and the name Tim written with a black permanent marker. After each game there was an X drawn on the ball for each win. In a regular year there would have been 9 or 10, but when the 14th X was carefully drawn on the ball, it became apparent that with only two home games remaining this was no regular year.

THE HOME STRETCH

With only two home games remaining in six seniors' careers, the week was about more than just getting two wins. The week was about sending the seniors out undefeated at home and building something for the underclassmen to continue the following year. There was a lot of reflection done throughout the course of the week. Every senior had experienced the ups and the downs of a college career and wanted to go out in a special way.

A match-up with last place Washington State seemed like a good place to start. Coming into the game WSU was without the services of two starters and all but mathematically eliminated from the conference tournament. Taking all of this into consideration, the last thing we wanted to do was underestimate a team that had nothing to lose. We prepared just like we would against a league leader, perhaps even more.

After a few days of light practice, game day finally arrived. During warm-ups it wasn't hard to tell that the WSU players would have rather been somewhere else than Mac Court. I think they sensed it might be a blowout before the game even began.

When the game started, we were a little sluggish, failing to put together much of anything on either end of the floor. Marcus Moore, who had blitzed us for 35 in Pullman, had begun the game trying to score even more. Our man-to-man defense didn't seem to be applying enough pressure, so after a brief discussion with the assistants, Coach Kent elected to go with our sporadically used match-up zone. The effects were immediate. Missed shots and turnovers quickly led to a 20-6 run and control of the game. Rid had caught fire and at one point scored eight straight to give us a 54-33 lead at the half.

The half was spent fine-tuning the few areas in which we had breakdowns we encountered in the zone. We realized that it could be a priceless weapon as we finished up the regular season and in the postseason. The second half was spent adding to WSU's misery, and things only got worse. We ended up shooting 72 percent from the field in the second half, including a jaw-dropping 13-of-17 from the three-point line on our way to a school record 16 three-pointers on only 26 attempts.

The final score, 115-77, broke a previous school record for points in a conference game, just missing the record for most points in any game. The 38-point margin was also a record against a conference opponent. With five players in double figures including a career-high of 25 points by Rid, all 12 players scored in the game for the first time all year. It was an offensive exhibition that surprised even us.

After the game it was all smiles, "We wanted to play hard and get the job done for our seniors because this is their last weekend at home. The best part of basketball is just playing, not worrying about anything and having fun, and we got to do that tonight," Rid said after the game with a grin.

Forward Robert Johnson wrapped the night up perfectly, "we came out ready to play because we know they can shoot the ball, and they were standing in our way of going 16-0 at home." Before leaving the locker room, Coach reminded us as usual to enjoy the win, but remember our biggest game was only two days away.

SENIOR NIGHT

It was bittersweet feeling as I walked into Mac Court for my final game as a player. I can only imagine that the five other seniors had many of the same feelings as I did. We all had our favorite moment, play, game, and plenty of heart-breaking stories. It felt good to be leaving a legacy behind with the promise of something special still to come, yet it was hard to believe we'd never run up and down the court with the name OREGON across our uniform.

Each of us had traveled a different path to get to the same place. Freddie was the blue chip recruit that Coach wanted to build his team around. Anthony was the productive transfer who was sure to have the offensive game that would fit into Coach's system. Chris was the 7-foot-2 project who had unbelievable upside. Kristian was the mentor to Chris that had a solid knowledge of the game. I was the transfer with three years to play that promised to do whatever I could to help win, wanting more than anything a chance to play at and against the highest level. Mark was another transfer who had traveled one of the most interesting paths of all of us and was also looking for a chance to contribute.

We had all arrived with different expectations, not sure what to expect but hoping to make a difference. With one game remaining it became clear that because we were playing one game for a chance to go undefeated at home, and head into the final week of the regular season in first place, we indeed had made a difference regardless of what happened that night or the week after.

"Whatever you have to do to win this game and send these seniors out undefeated, you do," Coach reminded us before the game.

It was clear that it was important to him, but I was more impressed by how important it was to the other players. They wanted to win the game not just because we were in the middle of a championship run, and a chance to go undefeated at home. Each underclassman wanted to send the seniors out the right way. Before the game that's all they talked about and after the game in the locker room you could feel their sincerity.

As for the game itself, Washington had already beaten us, and seemed confident and determined to duplicate the result. We had struggled to guard them and realized that unlike the WSU game this had the potential to go down to the wire.

A few minutes before tip-off, the players lined up as each senior and his parents were introduced and given a ceremonial rousing ovation. Along with being senior night it was also the last home game of the season, resulting in each player having a lot of family and friends in attendance. However, Freddie managed to out-do the entire team, struggling to find tickets to the sold-out game for the 20-plus family members who had traveled from as far Arkansas.

Freddie's family never missed a home game, and rarely a road game, but in the middle of the year his Dad was forced to travel back to Arkansas where his company was located and finish up a job. No one ever said anything, but we all knew it was tough for Freddie not to have his dad around. So when his Dad flew in for the last two games, we all expected a big performance. He had delivered as much as possible in the blowout win Thursday, so on the finale I thought he would take it to another level.

When the game began he didn't disappoint, scoring from everywhere and racking up 19 points in the first nine minutes. He was showing energy on every play that we had only seen flashes of, playing at a higher level than every other player on the floor, and putting on a show for more than just his family and friends who had made the long trip. By the end of the half he had scored 21 points including a dunk right on top of UW's Erroll Knight that brought the crowd to its feet and a brief celebration by Freddie. To our surprise this didn't rattle Washington one bit. The Huskies hung in and went on an 11-1 run to take the lead from us. We took the lead back on the next play when Rid hit a three, managing to coast into the half with a 51-45 lead.

When the second half started we again went on a run that Washington answered. The entire second half was back and forth; we would build a lead and UW would hit a couple of shots to stay in the game. With less than four minutes the Huskies had cut the lead to 77-71. The score was starting to get too close for comfort. Then appropriately on senior night, Freddie received a pass just outside the three-point line, and, as the ball slid off his fingertips, you could just feel it was going in. Again not backing down, UW cut the lead to three points before Rid penetrated and found Freddie again for another three that put the game out of reach with under a minute left.

Washington had given us all we could handle, shooting 54 percent from the field and 64 percent from the three-point line, both of which surpassed our percentages. Yet we had squeaked out a 90-84 win in front of an energetic sold out crowd that also featured Oregon quarterback Joey Harrington disguised in a beard and wig. Although the game was over the crowd stayed after to hear Coach Kent thank them as they cheered for the seniors and the underclassman who would carry the torch the next time they stepped onto the floor.

As the team stood huddled in front of the scorer's table it was hard not to cheer ourselves. Besides the brilliant 33-point, seven-rebound, five-steal performance of Freddie and the workman-like 23 point game of Jackson, we had accomplished something as a team. Part of that success came from the relentless support of the Mac Court faithful who stood there cheering for us as we cheered, thanking them for their support.

By winning our final home game we became the only team since 1938 to go undefeated at home. In addition to a place in the record books, we stood all alone in first place because of a USC loss. With one week to play in the conference, we were two games away from Oregon's first outright league title in 63 years. At 20-7 we had picked up only the ninth 20-win season in the school's history.

After all of our big wins Coach Graham would always say, "How about them Ducks?" as he gave everyone a high five outside the locker room doors. Although it was a little cheesy, it started to grow on me and I would always make a point of reminding him if he forgot. As I walked in after my last home game I beat him to it and found myself blurting out, "How about them Ducks?" as I strode in the locker room.

It was a satisfying feeling as we sat in the locker room, most likely failing to realize how big of an achievement it really is to not only go undefeated at home, but in one of the top conferences in the country.

Fully expecting Coach Kent to come in with a smile from ear to ear, I was caught off-guard when he walked in with a disappointing look on his face. "I want to apologize to the seniors who didn't get in," he said.

It was then that I realized what our team was made of. Every guy who didn't play was just as happy as the guys who did. Seldom do you get to a point as a team where you go beyond talking about giving up something for the team, and actually experience it. However, you could feel that the rewards of going undefeated at home and being in first place were more than just a sacrifice for the seniors who didn't play. Each player in the room had given up something of themselves for the sake of the team.

CHAPTER 9
The Biggest of the Biggest

"Victory belongs to the most persevering" — *Napoleon Bonaparte*

In a season that each game had become bigger than the last, we had finally arrived at the biggest game not only in the season, but one of the biggest games in the history of the school. Oregon had never won a PAC-10 championship and, for the program, this was easily one of the most important games in over 50 years. We had reached our goal of going undefeated at home and it wasn't difficult to switch gears onto a goal that had taken years to make a reality.

As usual we took Monday off, only showing up for a quick lift at the Casanova Center and an academic session afterwards. After each player met with a coach to make sure that his academics were in order, we were prepared to leave when we learned that Coach wanted to meet with us for a few minutes. There was a simple formula for Coach Kent's few minutes; take whatever length he claims it will be and multiple it by four!

We all assembled in the football film room, making sure that we were comfortable, fully expecting a 45-minute meeting. When Coach walked in he had a little box in his hand. As he passed it to Freddie who was in the seat by the door, everyone was amazed when the box's contents were revealed. Freddie gently slid a PAC-10 championship football ring out. The thing was huge and, similar to the sun, had the potential to blind you if you looked at it too long.

Luke Jackson always finding a way to score.

As a high school kid all I wanted was a championship ring, and when I had arrived at Oregon that same desire only intensified. I was not alone. Every guy in the room held the ring and, as each man examined its weight and design, you could see his very thoughts. Each guy was thinking about winning the championship and sliding a ring on with his name on the side. It took a good 20 minutes just to get the ring through everyone's hands. It had been awhile since I had wanted something as badly as I wanted one of those rings.

After collecting the ring, Coach talked about one thing, winning the PAC-10 championship. Our goal had felt so close to a reality when we had held that ring in our hands, you could tell that the three-day wait for the game was going to feel like an eternity.

If we beat USC on Thursday it was simple, we at least guaranteed ourselves a share of the title. However, if we lost, the picture became cloudy. We would still have the potential for a share of the title, but there would be no question that it would be shared with at least one other team and possibly two.

In 1991 Oregon State led by one game heading down to Arizona, needing a split to gain a piece of the conference title. In the Beaver's first game they beat Arizona State, assuring them at least a share, and with a sweep two days later, they had a chance for the outright title. However, the next game they played as though they had already won, and were defeated handily, thus placing a "Co-Champions" next to their name instead of "Champions."

MEDIA

I was always intrigued with the media. To start the season catching a highlight of one of our games on Sportscenter was all but impossible. It became clear that unless you were ranked in the top 25, or you were playing a team in the top 25, nobody really knew much about you. Breaking in to the top 25 is one of the strangest parts about the media, the majority of getting into the rankings is reputation, and how much you're on TV. It was interesting to watch through the course of the year how we slowly crept into the rankings and onto Sportscenter. Here we had one of the most explosive players in the country and for the first half of the year you had to live in Oregon to catch a highlight.

In the week leading up to the showdown in Tinseltown, the talk was suddenly about this upstart Oregon team that was surprising everyone. Dick Vitale, Digger Phelps and Jay Bilas were suddenly talking about the Ducks. It was strange to sit in a hotel room and hear someone on TV predict the outcome of the game you still hadn't played. Even though we had accomplished so much, people still didn't realize how good we were. We had been tagged a poor road team, and with our final two games on the road, there were only a select few, including our team, who thought we could actually get the sweep.

In the locker room Tuesday, Freddie was talking about a radio interview he had just concluded with Sean Salisbury, who was a USC alum, and Jason Jackson of ESPN radio. "I bet him that if we beat USC he would sing our fight song, and if we lost I would sing USC's," Freddie said with a smile. I was a little surprised, yet the bet that was all but a prediction by Freddie was certainly reassuring.

THE LUCKY COIN

The stage was set; the dramatics were in place. This was not just one team with a chance for a title playing another team. Both teams were playing for the conference crown; a win for us eliminated USC, and a win for USC put us in a must-win situation just to share the crown with two other teams. After a close home finale, everything was in order for our trip to Southern California. Everything except one thing, that is.

In the Washington game Rid had one of his worst games of the year, shooting an uncharacteristic 1-for-10 from the field, missing badly on several shots. He had taken a fall and had apparently jammed his wrist in the first half. But he claimed that the injury looked worse than it really was. Despite playing a great all-around game he had struggled to shoot the ball, and was visibly frustrated after the game.

That week in practice the frustration continued. Heading into the biggest game of his career his stroke was off. It's a difficult thing for a shooter when their shot is off. It's frustrating enough if it's in the summer, but two days before the biggest game of your career can be a little overwhelming.

No one said a word, but the reality was that, without Rid's shooting, our chances against USC on Thursday went down considerably. We could beat the Washington's, but a match-up for the title would require big games from everyone who stepped onto the floor. After both days of practice he had spent extra time trying to work the kinks out. "My stroke felt off. I wasn't worried as much as I was frustrated. It just felt funny so I finally told myself to forget it and move on" he later remembered.

As we met at the Casanova Center, preparing to board the team bus and head to the airport, my wife Joy dropped me off. As I told her goodbye she handed me a golden dollar that she had picked up at the bank that day. "For good luck" she said. Not being really superstitious, I put the coin into my pocket, told her thanks and kissed her goodbye.

In line at the airport I approached Rid to talk to him about his stroke. As a player there's nothing worse than feeling like your shots off, so I tried to give him some reassurance.

"What ya thinking?" I asked him.

" Not much" he unconvincingly replied.

I told him I had noticed that his shot was off and that he didn't need to worry about it. After all, in the 27 games we had played, he had shot the ball badly in one game. I jokingly told him some of my horror stories, and finally finished by telling him that I had a feeling that he was going to have a big game.

As he appeared to loosen up I pulled the golden dollar out of my shirt pocket and told him that it was lucky.

"Touch it," I said.

Unsure what the heck I was doing he quickly touched the coin with his fore finger.

"What was that," I asked with a chuckle.

"The coin is lucky; touch the thing with each finger on your shooting hand," I ordered.

As he touched the coin, I simply told him that his stroke was back.

Walking away I wondered to myself what the heck I was doing claiming the coin was lucky! But if nothing else it loosened him up, and that was something the whole team needed.

We had a great two days of practice that seemed more focused than usual. At the time I didn't know if that was a good thing or a bad thing. As we arrived that night, we headed to the Cheesecake Factory, a place that was becoming a team favorite for dinner.

That night we skipped walk-through, "we know what they do. We'll cover it again tomorrow in shoot-around," Coach said as we headed back to the hotel.

Without having to be told, everyone was in bed early, but none of us were getting much sleep. It's difficult, if not impossible, to not think about the biggest game of the season the night before.

When breakfast came around, we were surprisingly loose, joking around, perhaps more as therapy for the nerves of the game that day than anything else. Right after breakfast we departed to the Los Angeles Sports Arena for our shoot-around. The Sports Arena is the dirtiest arena we play in. It feels like the whole place could come down at any minute. The seats are old, the floor is slippery and the outside is a hideous aqua blue. I was always amazed at the thought of an NBA team, the Clippers, playing in the building just three years ago.

Much like WSU, if there were 3,000 fans at a game, that was a lot. However, this year we had heard reports that USC officials were going to sell the place out, which only added to the excitement. Probably the only thing that could ruin the atmosphere would be to show up for a game deciding the championship and have just a few thousand fans there.

Our shoot-around featured two things that day, a walk-through, and a lot of shooting around. Our game plan was simple, defend and shoot the ball well. In order to get the win we were going to have to stop them from getting big games from more than one or two guys. Similar to the game in Eugene, we knew that Clancy was going to score, but it always seems to be the other players who have the chance to beat us.

As we entered the arena and stepped onto the floor to stretch, I was watching Rid closely. I thought how he shot the ball in the shoot-around would be a good measure of how he was going to shot that night. After a few minutes of stretching, we started to get some shots up at both ends of the floor, switching ends after every five minutes.

When he put up his first shot I knew that his stroke was back, the flick of the wrist was back, and so was the net tingling result. I didn't say anything to him the rest of the shoot-around, but you could tell that things were back and the relief was apparent on his face as well as those of the coaches.

After the shoot-around, I walked up to him and nonchalantly said, "Shot looked pretty good today."

His response, not words, but a big smile and a nod of the head.

The rest of the day seemed to last forever; it felt like we had been in LA for a week, which usually isn't such a bad thing if it's sunny. Throughout the course of the day I asked just about everyone how they felt about the game. Trying to distract my nervous mind, I thought others' responses might do the trick.

QUIET CALM

Just before the game in the locker room there was a quiet calm, I don't think I realized the significance at the time, but there was certainly something different in the locker room. Most teams would have loved to wrap up the title two weeks into the season, but as I looked around at each person I felt strongly that this is what it was all about. As much pressure as there seemed to be surrounding the game, the locker room felt far removed. As I looked at Luke Jackson I had a feeling that this was exactly where he wanted to be, playing a game where everything was on the line.

No longer were the games a set up for the next game, this was it. After the ups and downs of an entire regular season where each game got bigger, we had finally reached the biggest. Looking around to Freddie, I felt confident that he felt the same way as Jackson, wanting nothing more than to be in LA playing for the Championship.

As I continued to look around the room I felt the same thing from each player. We had all come to Oregon with the hopes of playing for a Championship, and there we were almost unsure if the situation was real.

Coach was on top of his game as we met one last time before heading onto the floor. He always had a way of making you feel like no matter how difficult the game or the opponent was; there was only one outcome, an Oregon win. "You've worked hard to get to this position; there is no reason to be nervous" Coach said with a smile. After summarizing the game plan, he gathered himself and confidently said, "If you play hard and defend you'll be the PAC-10 Champions!"

SHOWDOWN IN TINSELTOWN

The game was not sold out, but it was probably as full as it had been since Michael Jordan and the Bulls played the Clippers there. More importantly it was loud; the student section even showed up a little early to give us a few words of discouragement. After the starting line-ups were announced, we huddled up for one last time before heading onto the floor. After a few words that I don't think anybody could actually hear, we teamed it up and, before Rid ran to half-court, I grabbed his arm, "you're going to play great," I said in one of my more serious tones.

When the game began both teams looked a little tight, I don't think it was as much being nervous as it was excited to play. We seemed a little caught off-guard when they scored on the first play, a Bluthenthal lay-up. However, within the next few minutes we had jumped all over them and led 11-4. Six of the 11 points had come on a pair of Ridnour threes, which was early proof that his stroke was back.

USC was not going to let us run away with the game, and fought back behind the explosive play of freshman guard Errick Craven. By the half USC had taken the lead back, 33-30. Neither team had played exceptionally well on the offensive end, but the defensive intensity by both teams had a lot to do with it. It had been one of our lowest scoring halves of the year.

In our locker room we felt pretty good about the position we were in. We were only down three points on the road and we had shot a horrible 37 percent from the field. Part of our offensive woes were apart of the uncommon 2-of-10 shooting of Freddie, and the inability of Luke Jackson to score a single point in the first half, something that never happened. Even though we were down three points, the locker room was full of confidence. We felt like we had them right were we wanted them. Coach Kent reminded us that at some point they would break, and sent us onto the floor by telling us this game might come down to the final minute.

In the second half everything seemed to go wrong, not only did our poor shooting continue, but we were also turning the ball over. With 11 minutes to play USC opened its biggest lead at 53-42. Then just when it felt like they would pull away, we scored a few baskets to keep us in the game. With less than 10 minutes to play we were still in striking distance, but were yet to have anybody catch fire.

Luke, who had finally scored eight minutes into the second half, had begun to get a little uneasy with the situation. Realizing the time slipping away, he took the ball and made what seemed to be a harmless move to the hoop, hanging just long enough to draw a foul from Sam Clancy. It seemed harmless until the announcer informed the crowd that it was Clancy's fourth foul. With over seven minutes left, there was no way USC Coach Henry Bibby could leave him on the floor.

In some games all it takes is one play to get back into the game. For us, this was the play. It not only brought the team back alive, but Luke Jackson. While Clancy was sitting on the sidelines we flashed our offensive prowess, blazing to a 56-55 lead while on a 12-2 run with six minutes left. Rid had struggled after the two early threes, but added another big shot that was a part of the run. Clancy re-entered the game and, with only a few minutes gone, had changed the momentum again. However, with us leading by one-point 60-59, Rid came down the floor, and let another fast break three fly from almost the exact spot of the floor as the back-breaking three in Eugene. The three had given us a 63-59 lead, and it felt like we were going to pull out the win after Freddie added a lay-up to make it 65-59.

However as we came upon the final minutes, Cravin, who had held the fort for USC in the first half, dribbled down the left side and nailed a long three pointer to put the Trojans within three. This wouldn't have been a problem, but on the next possession we turned the ball over, and gave USC chance to tie the game with less than a minute remaining.

After a timeout, USC patiently worked the ball around and began to set up a play that gave David Bluthenthal a three at the top of the key. It looked like the same play they ran in Eugene. Bluthenthal had struggled all game, going scoreless since the first play of the game. However, when he caught the ball I had a bad feeling. As he got in rhythm and let the shot go, the result only reinforced it. As the ball dropped through the net, all 12,000 fans rose to their feet, with the game tied 65-65.

With half a minute remaining, we dribbled to half court and called a timeout to set up the final play. The huddle was calm; Coach made it clear that we wanted the last shot, avoiding the disaster that had lost the Portland game early on. The plan was to run our motion to get the clock down to 10 seconds and then whoever had the mismatch would try and make a play.

It was official, I had never been as nervous as I was in those final 30 seconds in my entire life. As we in-bounded the ball, USC seemed content with having the game come down to the final shot. All the Trojans sat back like they were waiting for us to make the first move. And when Freddie realized he had the slower Bluthenthal on him, he motioned for the ball. It then became clear to me that there was no question who was going to take the last shot. Standing 40 feet from the basket Freddie glanced at the clock, then the court, as he waited for the clock to reach 10 seconds.

Glancing one more time at the clock, he got set and started to make his move, taking a few dribbles to get some breathing room. Then he turned on the jets, driving right past Bluthenthal, and a confused Granville who didn't know whether to help or step in front of Freddie. By the time he decided it was too late, Freddie had already left the ground and, as Clancy came over to pressure the shot, Freddie hung in the air just long enough to gather himself.

As the ball left his hand, the whole world seemed to stop and it looked like it was just Freddie out there in slow motion. As the ball neared the rim the crowd went silent. The ball gently slid over the rim, as it fell through the net as softly as it had left his hand.

The crowd was stunned, and, to be honest, so were we. With time running out, USC desperately inbounded the ball to Granville who got as close to half court before throwing up the Trojans' final hope. The ball slammed off the backboard, coming uncomfortably close to going in before it bounced on the floor as the horn sounded. Shocked I checked the score to make sure I wasn't hallucinating, Oregon 67 USC 65. The clock read 00:00.

Realizing we had just won the game I jumped on my seat and hugged somebody before almost falling off. Then we all ran onto the floor hugging and high-fiving anyone with Oregon on their jersey.

As we celebrated briefly, we gathered on the floor, huddled up and said the Lord's Prayer as we had done after every win and every loss! As we finished, we went right back to celebrating. I ran into Athletic Director Bill

Moos on the way off the court, "I told you" I said referring to discussions earlier in the year about the basketball and football teams winning PAC-10 Championships in the same year.

"You told me," he simply replied.

When we finally arrived in the locker room there was something written on the board that I will never forget. <u>Congratulations, PAC-10 Champions</u>! The reason I will never forget it was not because of what it necessarily said, but when it was written. When we stepped into the locker room, Coach Kent had yet to enter, when he did I realized that it had been written long before Freddie's last-second shot, It had been written at the half by Coach Kent after the players went back onto the floor.

It feels awkward that I was so amazed by something so simple, but it seemed to tell the story of our season. We were a team, players and coaches who firmly believed we could win the PAC-10 Championship. At the half, down three and in the midst of the toughest game of the year, Coach Kent believed so much that we were going to win the championship that he wrote it on the board 20 minutes before the game was over.

I put it in to perspective when I pictured walking into the locker room after a loss and finding the same phrase on the board. Luke Ridnour only confirmed my thought weeks later, "I knew we were going to win; there was just that feeling, whether it was something in practice or what, it was there and every guy could feel it!"

When Coach Kent walked in the door, he said, "We're not doing anything until I see the dance." I had already been at the front of the room with my back to the team ready to pull it out one last time. After a few sumo steps and karate chops, I foolishly finished with a break-dancing spin that gave me a massive carpet burn. As I stood up it was official, we were the PAC-10 Champions!

When you talk so much about achieving something special, you create a picture in your mind of exactly what it will be like. However, when you actually accomplish the feat, it always feels different than you thought, I guess that's what makes accomplishments feel so great. After a few words regarding closing the deal two days later at UCLA, the celebration had begun.

As Freddie, Luke, and Rid met with the media, Jay Anderson and I had different plans. With the actual championship ring months away from arriving, we decided to create our own rings to commemorate the occasion. We decided to apply athletic tape with an "O" and PAC-10 Champs around our fingers, not quite 24k gold, but for the night it would do.

The game had been meaningful on so many different levels; it's hard to pick one. Not only was it a great college basketball game, that had record-breaking magnitude, but it had broken the limits placed on our team before and during the year. It was also won on a last-second shot by a player who had finally broken the label of inconsistent and as an underachiever. I think most of all it was the perfect example of what our team was all about.

Perhaps the evidence lies not in the product but by the words of the players who produced it, "We just kept fighting, never giving up by staying with each other the whole time. Every time there was a timeout or a huddle on the floor, you could see it in everyone's eyes. There wasn't any panic; we just kept being positive, knowing that we just needed to weather the storm and give ourselves a chance at the end," Luke Ridnour remembered.

This was indeed a rare team. "The best part about the game was that it was a team championship; everyone contributed, even the guys that didn't play. I remember Jay kept coming up to me in timeouts telling me to keep shooting, that it would start to fall. Every guy on and off the court was positive," Rid sincerely put it weeks after it had set in.

Rid wasn't the only one who recognized the effects of a strong team, "The road is a hostile environment, but if you stick together, you can pull of things like this," James Davis said after the game.

In 1945 the University of Oregon shared the Pacific Coast Conference Northern Division title with Washington State. That title was the last time that Oregon had won or shared a conference title in 57 years! Even hours after the game the reality still had not set in. One reason was the game Saturday against UCLA; that with a win would give us sole possession of the championship. The other was that our team still had a goal and the championship had only intensified that.

After the game there was a great deal of celebration with teammates, friends and families. We headed to none other than the CheeseCake Factory to celebrate the victory. There was an incredible feeling of satisfaction that night, all the hard work and time had paid off. After winning the championship, I was surprised how difficult it really was. I thought back over the season game by game, thinking about how we progressively became better and better, until finally becoming a championship team.

Every win and loss had taught us an important lesson that was used in the game against USC. The sweep at home versus the Arizona teams showed us how good we could be. The win down there was even more convincing, then the loss to ASU showed us what could happen if we got ahead of ourselves. The sweep at home against Cal and Stanford proved to us that we would need more than our offense to win, ultimately winning each game with defense down the stretch.

The OSU game forced us to play an unfamiliar style and find a way to win. At Washington we had to be reminded that we were not only the team to beat, but also that it didn't matter how many points you scored if the other team scored more. When we played WSU two days later, we learned how to rebound quickly and grind out a tough win on the road.

When we played UCLA and USC at home, we learned how to put a game away when we had to. Against USC we learned one of the most important lessons, which was finding a way to win. The next week in the Bay Area, we were given a painful real game example of how on the road you have to be even more mentally focused. In the final game of the Civil War, we discovered a new dimension of our defense. In the Washington State game, we weathered the storm and put the game out of reach. In our final home game against Washington, we took a team's very best shot and never panicked. We had indeed traveled a long road to a championship!

FINISH WHAT WE STARTED!

The idea of sharing the title didn't sit well with us as we woke up the next morning. With a loss to Stanford, Arizona had been eliminated from contention, along with USC. With a win over ASU, Cal was now a victory over Arizona and a loss from us from sharing our title. Although we would know the outcome of the Cal-Arizona game before our game was finished, our goal from the start was to be in control of our own destiny by getting the sweep.

The day after the USC game I realized how much pressure there really was on the game. It felt like the weight of the world had been lifted off our shoulders. With a match-up with UCLA the next day we were relaxed and confident that we were going to finish what we started.

On the way to practice that day I noticed Freddie on a cell phone, again smiling. When he got off the phone I asked what that was all about, "Oh, just Sean Salisbury singing the Oregon fight song," he replied. This brought a smile to my face as I sat there and visualized him singing our fight song to a nationwide ESPN radio audience. I felt a few minutes of satisfaction.

In a night where there was so much to be excited and happy about, there had been one downside to the win against USC. In the second half, James landed awkwardly on Brian's knee. The early prognosis was that the injury would require surgery, but there was an outside chance he could return to limited action in three weeks, which would have been well into the NCAA tournament. It was a tough weekend for him. He related a story about wanting to play in the NCAA tournament ever since he was a kid, and said that he was going to play regardless of how badly the knee was hurt.

The day of the game arrived and, with an afternoon tip-off, the wait was unbearable. When we warmed-up there was something different; we had the confidence of champions. Each team had approached our game like we were the team to beat. As we stepped onto the floor, every guy believed that from here on out we were the team to beat.

Before tip-off, we all met in the locker room. Coach Kent had written a ton of stuff on the board, and, as he began to cover all the information, he realized that we were no longer the same team that we had once been. After covering a few strategies, he suddenly put the chalk down and said, "Play this game for your parents, so we can stay in the West for the NCAA tournament and they can afford to get there." He was referring to the brackets that two years ago sent us to Buffalo, New York, for the first round unaccompanied by parents who couldn't make the long trip cross-country.

To everyone's surprise we got up, teamed it up and went onto the floor without so much as talking about the details of the game plan. Coach Kent did a lot of different things, but one thing he never did was skip chalk talk.

The best part about playing UCLA is Pauley Pavilion. When you look up and see all the national championship banners hanging and then glance into the crowd and see John Wooden attentively watching the game, you can't help but feel the sense of history. The fact that the game was near capacity and was on national TV (CBS), made it even better.

The start of the game was not pretty, UCLA looked uninterested, and we looked tired. However, about 10 minutes into the game the intensity finally picked up. In the first half we had a few chances to pull away, but fatigue and missed shots prevented us from taking more than a 37-31 lead into the locker room at the half.

Although Arizona was blowing out Cal, essentially giving us sole possession of the title, we now looked at the game from the standpoint of proving a point and helping our seeding in the NCAA tournament. At the half we looked like a tired prizefighter, but once again we were determined to finish what we started.

We came out expecting UCLA to pick up its intensity, but the Bruins still seemed unsure of what they were trying to get done. We worked our way to another lead, when UCLA coach Steve Lavin abruptly put his starters on the bench with 13 minutes left in the game, finally realizing what we had noticed from the start of the game.

Before we knew what had happened, UCLA now led 49-48. After a timeout and a few timely threes by James and Rid, we managed to get the lead back, but along with the lead we also had another close game. After trading punches over the next few minutes, UCLA found center Dan Gadzuric on the free throw line with 42 seconds left for a chance to tie the game. Because he made only one, we had a one-point lead and the ball.

Once again we ran our motion to take some time off the clock. This time it was clear that we would attack without the use of a timeout. So, with the shot clock running down, we went to who else but Freddie Jones. After a game-winning shot two days earlier, it only made sense. Freddie received the ball on the left side, right in front of our bench. After giving a few fakes, he penetrated into the middle, finding himself right in front of 6-11 Dan Gadzuric with nowhere to go. As he jumped into the air, Freddie realized

Gadzuric was going to block his shot and give the Bruins a chance to win at the other end. So in the split second he was in the air, he knocked the ball off Gadzuric's arm, landed on the ground as he snatched the ball out of the air and rolled the ball up and over the rim for the basket and a three-point lead.

Although not as dramatic as the game-winning shot at USC, it was still an impressive shot at the right time. UCLA went down the floor looking for a tie and a chance to send the game into overtime. But after struggling to get a good look, the Bruins were forced to settle for a jumper from freshman guard Ryan Walcott. When his shot missed, we rebounded the ball as time expired. We had finally finished what we started, and along the way picked up our first win at Pauley Pavilion since 1984.

In an arena where so many championships had been won, we huddled at half court as the official PAC-10 Champions, finally winning one of our own. To our surprise Hud had some PAC-10 Championship hats made up and, before we knew it, we all had shiny white "Oregon, PAC-10 Basketball Champion" hats.

As we huddled up to again offer a prayer of thanks, we got together and yelled "PAC-10 Champs," looking at one another with a smile, realizing that it had a pretty nice ring to it.

THE TRIP HOME

After the game the plan was to go straight to the airport and be back in Eugene by 10:30 p.m. So, after interviews and mingling with friends and family who made the trip, we jumped onto the bus and made our way to the airport. On the bus we were talking about printing up some T-shirts, and I asked Coach Kent if Kristian and I could do the design. I fully expected to be denied, but without thinking twice he said, "Sure, give the designs to Hud."

The trip back was spent talking about the game and the season. Reality was months away from setting in, but we still tried to enjoy the significance of the victory. That night a lot of guys asked each other, "Can you believe we just won the PAC-10 title?" We had focused and believed all year that we were going to win the PAC-10 championship, yet there we sat finding it difficult to believe we finally did.

As our bus pulled up to the Casanova parking lot someone yelled, "Look at all those people." I thought someone was joking around so I continued to lie down until I looked up as everyone looked out the right side of the bus. When I finally looked out the window, I was amazed at what I had saw.

There in the parking lot at the Casanova center stood about 350 people at 11:15 at night in the cold and rain. As we turned into the parking lot the Duck mascot directed the bus into its proper place. When the door opened, you could hear the roar of the crowd and, as each person stepped off the bus, a cheer went out. For about 25 minutes we all felt like a movie star stepping out of a limousine. When everyone finally got off the bus chants of, "Let's go, Ducks" went out among the crowd.

Throughout the year I constantly found myself amazed with the support of Duck athletics, but that night, you really could really feel the appreciation our fans had. Young and old had gathered there in the cold, probably waiting over an hour for our arrival. As they stood and cheered for us, the appreciation and support was more than mutual.

CAREFUL WHAT YOU WISH FOR!

With the conference title wrapped up, and ranked No. 9 in the country, it was important that we switch gears once again. With the re-instated PAC-10 Tournament, our next goal was again waiting for us down in LA, this time a week later in the Staples Center. With the win against USC we had clinched the number one seed in the tournament, and also a third match-up with the Huskies. After our last game with them, they openly talked about a potential re-match in the conference tournament.

"We match up well with them; we're just as athletic as them. A lot of people are hoping we'll get that match-up down there," Washington guard Curtis Allen said a week before the seeds were determined. After we had beaten them in Eugene, they seemed to be saying all the wrong things. Usually you give the winning team credit for the victory and talk about what you needed to do differently after a loss. Even after we were embarrassed early in the year at Portland by a lesser team, we still gave them credit. Although we were the better team, Washington still seemed to be confused between the difference in first and eighth place.

"I wouldn't say there are mismatches any more…the teams in the PAC-10 are so closely matched," forward Doug Wrenn said in reference to Oregon and Washington. Guard Curtis Allen even had the nerve to add, "If we can get them in L.A., that would be great." Throughout the second half of the year we continually felt like we weren't getting the respect we deserved. The comments from the Washington players and coaches only seemed to confirm our feelings.

Washington had a record of 11-17 overall, and 5-13 in the conference, while we took a 23-7, 14-4 record into the tournament. Even though the Huskies couldn't recognize the difference between the two, we were deter-mined to go down to L.A. and show them. They had asked for the match-up, not knowing that we were even happier to oblige.

After a few days of practice, we were on our way back down to L.A. for the second straight week. Part of the conference tournament festivities included an awards banquet on Wednesday, the night before the tournament started. This was not only where they were going to hand out the year's conference awards, but also induct a former player from each conference school into the PAC-10 hall of fame. Some of the inductees in attendance included the great John Wooden, our very own John Dick, Pete Newell, and the keynote speaker, Sean Elliot.

The banquet was well done, but from the very start it had the potential to go three hours or more. This didn't sit well with many coaches or players who had to play the very next day. Especially our team, with a game time of 1:15 in the afternoon the next day, rest seemed more important than spending three hours at a banquet.

There wasn't a whole lot of excitement other than giving Oregon great John Dick an ovation. However, when the player of the year and the all-conference teams were announced, the room was paying close attention. After two game-winning shots, one of which was for the PAC-10 title, I thought for sure Freddie would receive player of the year. Sitting as a team in the back of the room, we paid attention as they read off each player's name. I nervously asked those around me if they thought Freddie would win. Then I found out that a lot of the coaches turned in their ballots before we even headed down to play USC and UCLA.

This was bad news, because everyone in the conference except for our team thought USC was going to beat us and win the title, thus it only made sense to give the award to the dominating Sam Clancy.

Along with the player awards, there was also the Coach of the Year award. Similar to the other awards, I felt that Coach Kent might be overlooked, and the award given to a Henry Bibby from USC, or an Olsen from Arizona. However, when they announced Coach Kent as the Coach of the Year, I felt that perhaps the rest of the conference hadn't overlooked our accomplishments.

They announced the all-conference team first including the players that were up for the player of the year. When I finally heard, "Luke Ridnour from the University of Oregon" my excitement grew, assuming that we were going to have at least two players on the all-conference team. Moment's later Freddie's name was also announced. Then, my heart sank as they announced, "The winner of the PAC-10 conference player of the year award goes to, Sam Clancy from USC."

Although everyone on our team felt strongly that Freddie was the Player of the Year, we found no reason to dwell on what should have been. Much like we had done all year, we joined the applause and congratulated our players and Coach who had been honored. Not one guy on the team went without approaching Rid, Freddie, Coach Kent, or Luke Jackson who had picked up second team, to tell them congratulations.

YOU JUST MIGHT GET IT...

With an afternoon tip-off, game day went by fairly fast, we skipped the shoot-around because it required that we wake up earlier than desired. So after sleeping in, and getting a good breakfast, we had a team meeting, and a brief walkthrough.

"This tournament will be preparation for the NCAA tournament," Coach Kent started off by saying. "Just like the NCAA, if you lose, you go home," he added.

Just like we had done all year, we looked at the situation in terms of how can we use the experience to help us get better and closer to our next goal. Well, our next goal was to win the conference tournament, but even more importantly getting to the Final Four. So with the pressure of lose and go home, we wanted to be aware, but also be comfortable with the pressure. Why, because the following week it would be the exact same.

As we made our way to the Staples Center, home of the NBA's Lakers and Clippers, the excitement was visible on everyone's faces. The re-birth of the conference tournament seemed to remind us of our past experiences in our high school state tournaments. With the number one seed came the number one locker room, the one the Lakers use. When we were informed of our designated locker room, everyone thought the coaches were just trying to add to the excitement. However, when the door opened and I looked down a long hall that had pictures from all of the championships on the walls, it didn't take long to be convinced.

The place looked like a fancy country club, the carpet had been covered with a foam-like cover, and the players names had been removed from above their lockers, but it was still obvious that the defending NBA champions made their home there. As I made my way down the hall, there were Magic, Kareem, West, Worthy, and, of course, Shaq and Kobe on the walls either gliding through the air, or holding a giant championship trophy. I hadn't even arrived into the main area and I was already excited.

Instead of the usual steel lockers in many of the other locker rooms, each player had an open area that looked more like a closet made out of a dark cheery wood. Most of the first 15 minutes was spent trying to figure out where Shaq, and Kobe sat. Once the excitement wore off, we began to stretch and get loose for the game that was an hour and a half away.

In the locker room in Mac Court, we all sit in the same place every time. It doesn't matter if we are meeting for 30 seconds or 30 minutes, we still sit in the same spot every time. Throughout the course of the year this was something that had begun to come along on each road trip with us. Each time we came into the locker room we would reorganize the chairs into the same half circle facing the dry erase board as we had at Mac. I don't know if we thought it was good luck, but nobody questioned it either.

Preparing for this game was easy. We had played them twice, the second time only been two weeks prior, and most importantly we felt disrespected, feeling we owed them more than just a loss, but a blowout. After we had gone through our regular warm-ups I went down to the other end of the floor where they were shooting around. I sat on the bench, and just wanted to watch them for a few minutes to try and get a feel for how ready they were to play the game.

You can tell a lot about a team and a player by how they warm-up. I remember a coach telling me one time that he could tell more about a player before the game started than watching him play an entire game. As I watched Washington shoot-around, I hoped the coach was wrong because Washington looked like they were set on backing up their ridiculous statements from the newspapers. Each player looked confident and comfortable, and, after losing the first game and struggling to beat them in the second, I hoped we were as ready to play as we appeared.

The first half was not what we had expected, Washington was serious about the claims they had made, and 15 minutes into the game they seemed to be correct. With a 31-18 lead, with less than six minutes to play, we had found ourselves playing poorly and facing the largest deficit of the season. Not only was Washington playing well, but it appeared easy. As I sat there on the bench I briefly contemplated the consequences of a first round upset to the eighth-seeded team. Our seeding in the NCAA tournament was in serious jeopardy. As unfair as it was, a loss probably meant the difference between playing in the West and playing in the East.

Unable to really get anything going, we were able to cut the lead to seven points at the half, 42-35. Before the coaches came into the locker room, the players did all the talking.

"If we lose, we go home," somebody yelled. "They're playing harder than we are," Rid added. When Coach walked into the room, as usual it went quiet.

"Well," he sighed, "we need to clean up a few things." Although it felt like everything went wrong, Coach Kent was determined to not let us panic. After reading a few statistics it was simple — they shot 54 percent and we shot 43 percent. We needed to play better and harder on defense, and needed to relax and shoot the ball on offense.

When we began the second half, we appeared to have steadied the ship. Then only 28 seconds into the half the shot clock suddenly malfunctioned. After workmen appeared to fix it, the clock again went off. Finally each team was called over to its bench while the problem was fixed. After about 15 minutes of sitting around, the shot clock was finally fixed for good.

Along with the shot clock, our first half problems were also fixed. Within the next five minutes we had gone on a 12-3 run, and regained the lead. Just like we had done all year, our ability to score quickly caught our opponent off guard and, by the time they realized what was happening, we were in control of the game.

Washington made a final push with less than 10 minutes to go, getting as close as 61-55, but this once again sparked our offensive fire as we worked our way towards a twenty-point lead. Before the game Freddie had a 102-degree fever, and we had wondered if he could play. He shook it off to score a solid 15 points. Luke Jackson picked up the slack, finishing with 27 points and a thunderous two-hand dunk that caused him to slide off the rim and crash to the ground on his back, with more pain to his pride than anything else. After playing a terrible first half that endangered our postseason future, we put things out of hand, walking away with an 86-64 blowout that we had talked about during the days leading up to the game. I wondered after the game if the Huskies were still happy with the match-up they had hoped for a few weeks ago!

As the final horn sounded, the Huskies looked stunned, and they had reason to be. We had outscored them 51-22 in the second half, forcing them to shoot 25 percent from the floor. The most satisfying part was the way we beat them. They had played well in the first half, but in the second half they were no match for our offense or our defensive pressure.

It felt good to get the first round win, yet there was still a lot of work to do. After our game we sat in the stands to watch the first half of the USC-Stanford game that determined our opponent. By this time, the 20,000 plus seats of the Staples Center had begun to fill up for the hometown Trojans. Stanford's players had made it clear earlier in the week that they weren't excited about the tournament and the problems it raised for their academic schedules. By the end of the first half, their play closely resembled their non-excitement about being in LA.

It was obvious at the half that USC was going to win, and by the time we were on our way to dinner, the Trojans had won by 25. I had read about Stanford's unhappiness, but thought maybe it was lip service. However, when we got back from dinner and Stanford had already packed and left for the airport, I realized they weren't fooling around.

For dinner that night, Hud decided to try this fancy seafood restaurant a few blocks from the hotel in downtown LA. The place was really nice, in fact they had the best shrimp I had ever tasted. By the kitchen they had this giant tank that had all the lobster and crab in it. A few of us went back there to check it out, and were surprised to find a crab that looked like something out of a bad 70's horror movie. This thing was huge; its body was probably a foot in diameter, and with its legs fully extended around four feet wide. The price tag, $ 250.000!

When I conveyed my surprise to the waiter, he told me something even more surprising; the amount of meat after cooking was eight pounds. After trying to convince Hud we should get at least two, I settled for a steak!

After heading back to the arena to watch the Arizona-ASU game, we met back at the hotel to cover the game the next day. When we showed up, Coach Duncan had written about a hundred things on a dry erase board. Coach Kent came in looked at the board and said, "Scott, we only played them a week a go." After spending a few minutes reviewing there personnel, and plays, we teamed it up and headed to our rooms.

When I got to my room there was a message flashing on the room phone. Confused that anyone had our room number, I played the message. I started to laugh when I heard the voice of Arizona player Luke Walton trying to find out if there was anyone who wanted to come to his room and play cards for money. Glancing over at the clock that read 11:34, I wondered what kind of guy calls a random room and leaves a message like that about playing cards. The next day I found out that he had talked to Rid about playing cards, and didn't realize that Rid and I had switched rooms.

SOMETHING OUT OF NOTHING

The ridiculous pre-game chatter didn't stop with Washington. When we met for breakfast the day of the game, USC's comments in the day's paper had also joined us. USC's players were back to talking about how they owed us a loss, and how we had stolen the conference title, and the coach of the year from them and their coach. This however, was far from the truth, and win or lose we had the feeling that USC would continually carry its bad attitude farther than the game with us. It was obvious that the Trojans were having withdrawal from the lost championship the week before, and were trying to transform a semifinal game in the conference tournament back into the conference championship!

I thought to myself that it was a good thing that the media wasn't asking me what I thought about the third match-up with USC. It would not have been difficult for me to tell them the degree of USC's poor sport mentality.

Humility is something that some teams just don't have, and when they don't win the big games, they afterwards complain about how they were slighted in some way.

Our team was a prime example of how to win and lose with class. There was an unwritten rule after our games that whether you win or lose, you always give the other team credit. Even if we knew the other team was outmatched the entire game we would talk about how hard they played or how they made us step up our level of play. There was never anything to gain by showing up an opponent, even if its players deserve it.

Our team wanted nothing more than to beat USC by 30 in front of 20,000 people, but we knew that our goal was more important than that one game, and any kind of win would be more than acceptable. Before the game Freddie was still dealing with the flu and fever that had plagued him for the last few days. However, there was no way he was going to miss a game like this. After going through the usual routines before the game, we were ready to begin.

Nearly every seat was filled, the majority with USC fans, and a few Arizona and Cal fans who were early for the next game featuring the two teams. Even a few stars showed up, Kevin Costner sat directly across from our bench, but appeared to be cheering for the Trojans. For the first tournament in over 10 years, so far it seemed to be a success.

Our game plan hadn't changed since the win a week ago, and once again we knew it was going to come down to limiting the production of their big three and not letting one of the other players have a career night on us. With our second game in as many nights, and Freddie being under the weather, Coach wanted to make sure that our energy level was there to start the game. The last thing we wanted was to have USC start the game on a tear because behind the energy of the crowd and their self-proclaimed revenge they owed us.

In the first half, the revenge USC had popped off about seemed to still be back at the Sports Arena across town. Flying up and down the floor as we had done all season, we were putting on a show for the opposing crowd that found it difficult to resist cheering for the spectacular play after play. With less than three minutes to play and leading 44-31, we were threatening to run away with the game. Then, as quickly as we had built the lead, USC had used a 14-4 run to close the gap to 48-45 at the half.

Although USC had turned a potential blowout into a close game, we still felt good about a three-point lead at the half. When the second half began USC and the crowd had not forgotten the momentum they had built before halftime. For the first 10 minutes, both teams tried to gain the upper hand. With a little over nine minutes to play Freddie picked up his fourth foul. He had been playing great and so far in the second half was our only player who was able to get anything going offensively. Worried about a possible fifth and final foul, Coach was forced to take him out. This was no doubt a problem for us, giving USC an early advantage.

However, a few minutes after Freddie had picked up his fourth, newly crowned player of the year Sam Clancy also picked up his fourth. There was a sigh of relief on our bench, Clancy had been equally as effective as Freddie, and this looked to even things out while he was out.

We fully expected USC Coach Henry Bibby to pull him out, but he acted as though it was Clancy's first foul, leaving him in the game with over seven minutes to play. This ended up being the turning point of the game. Bibby had taken a gamble, and it had paid off. Clancy and the Trojans steamrolled to an 80-71 lead with five minutes to play, forcing Coach Kent to put Freddie back in the game.

By this time USC had control of the game and was executing a trapping defense that was forcing uncharacteristic turnovers from just about every player on the floor. We had begun to feel the effects of back-to-back games and a tough road trip less than a week behind us. Without ever giving up, we were beaten, the last few minutes were never close and we finished with an 89-78 loss.

The last few minutes ended as tasteless as the comments they made in the papers. Their players were talking trash, and jumping up and down as though they had won the championship. We had been beaten, not by a better team, but instead, by a team that played hard and was able to get a few breaks at the right times of the game. They had done a good job of forcing turnovers, tying our season high of 21. They had also received a big lift from sporadic players Desmon Farmer and Jerry Dupree. In the end they had six players in double figures, getting the kind of big game performances they needed from each player.

As we sat in our locker room, we were stunned. After a six game win streak, that had spanned almost a month, we had forgot how bad it hurt to lose. We had a great chance to win the game, but had failed to capitalize at the right times. Instead of our defense being the culprit, it was our offense that had turned the ball over, giving them a number of easy lay-ups that helped put the game out of reach.

The problem with turning the ball over is that it not only gives the ball to the other team in a position where it can score easily, but you also fail to get a shot off on offense. This obviously makes it difficult to score if you can't shoot the ball. We had done a good job the entire year of controlling the game with our superb ball handling and precise passing, and with the loss we were forced to experience the consequences.

After talking about the loss, it didn't take long for Coach Kent to shine a positive light on the situation. "You've gone 16-0 at home, and you're the PAC-10 Champions," he said. "More importantly, this thing isn't over; we are heading home to a wonderful celebration at Mac Court, and the NCAA tournament." Although we all knew the season was far from over, it was still going to take a few days to forget the loss.

After the game we were given the opportunity to spend some time with our families before meeting back at the hotel for the next day's itinerary. The next day was spent traveling back to Eugene and getting some rest. The next afternoon I watched the championship game between USC and Arizona at home. USC had led most of the game, but Arizona pulled away in the second half, winning without much excitement.

There were a few minutes of satisfaction as I saw the USC players leave the floor with different expressions than they had worn the night before. I wondered if they still thought we stole the championship from them after the Arizona loss, or if they finally realized that wee had won it.

CHAPTER 10
Selection Sunday

"Glory gives herself only to those who always dreamed of her" — *Charles de Gaulle*

Describing the excitement and uncertainty before you find out where and whom you'll be playing in the NCAA tournament is difficult. As a kid growing up, March Madness and the NCAA tournament, is the ultimate dream of a basketball player. There is no other college or professional playoff system that can duplicate the wild games and cutthroat brackets. In a year where the BCS took a great deal of deserved criticism in football, the field of 64 was once again ready to provide last-second wins, and improbable underdog victories that remind us of how great the college game is.

The first order of business is selecting the teams. This is where the always-interesting brackets are revealed to the disappointed and the relieved. Full of surprises and burst bubbles, Selection Sunday always promises to provide water cooler talk the next day as brackets are filled out and pools are formed.

With the PAC-10 Championship still unofficially celebrated, a Selection Sunday party at Mac Court provided an opportunity to cut down the nets, and celebrate our berth in the NCAA tournament. Before the party started, we met in the locker room to cover the day's schedule and, most importantly, to get refocused on the task at hand after a tough loss.

JC transfer Brian Helquist provided muscle and scoring off the bench.

Although we were only two days removed from the USC loss, we had again done what we had all year, found away to learn from the loss. At this point in the season the thought of repeatedly turning losses into positives had begun to seem a little ridiculous. However, we had realized that the tournament win over Washington and loss to USC had been a valuable lesson for the upcoming NCAA tournament.

It wasn't difficult to also realize that another loss and the season was over for good. The conference tournament had prepared us for the win or go home atmosphere that the NCAA tournament was all about. We didn't learn that we needed to play better defense, or get better shots, something we had been learning all season. Instead we got a feel of the pressure of tournament time, and what it took to win and lose. Each loss throughout the year had prepared us for a certain game. The loss to USC was no different; the idea that a loss in the conference tournament could help us get to the Final Four seemed to be acceptable, but only after a few days.

We had all had a few days to get over the loss, but the overall attitude of the team was concern. Not so much because of the play in the loss, but instead the potential effects the second round conference tournament loss could have on our seeding. We had struggled all year to gain respect, and felt that the selection committee was going to hold the loss against us with a poor seed. With a conference tournament win, we could have locked up a No. 2 seed, but felt sure that we could slip as far as a No. 5.

Before having to worry about seeding, it was time to celebrate, and with the post-season still ahead of us, there was still more than enough to celebrate. With about 3,500 fans in attendance, we lined up in the hall as we were announced as, "the 2001-2002 PAC-10 Champions," we walked onto the floor amid a standing ovation.

There were three giant TV screens in front of the crowd that would be showing the selection process on CBS. We sat in a row of chairs directly in front of the screens. As each player's name was called we made our way to the basketball hoops at each end to cut down a piece of the nets. In the meeting before the celebration, Coach Kent had asked us if there were any questions regarding the ceremony. Freddie raised his hand and said, "I've never won anything; how do you cut down the nets?"

I thought he was joking, but after the laughter died down, and he still had a serious look on his face, everyone reassured him that there was nothing to it.

Each player was given a rousing applause as we cut down a keepsake from the championship run. The final two people were Coach Kent and Freddie. As they walked to opposite ends the crowd went crazy as they snipped down the rest of the net.

After the nets were cut down a highlight video was shown, with just enough time for Coach Kent to give a speech before the selection show on CBS began. Each year CBS broadcasts live footage from a number of team's selection parties. This year CBS picked us as one of those schools. When the CBS selection show began, the cameras cut to live footage from Mac Court, and there we were, looking right back at ourselves on the screen.

As the show began, we sat there anxiously awaiting the announcement of our name. After a few commercial breaks, our name was finally announced: "the number two seed in the Midwest, OREGON." As the live footage switched to Mac Court, every player and fan jumped up in astonishment. It felt too good to be true. We were hoping for a No. 3 seed, and expecting a 4 or 5. When they announced that we would be just eight hours down the road playing Montana, the excitement grew even more.

There was a sharp contrast to two years ago when we were sent to Buffalo as an 8 seed. We had finished ahead of UCLA in the conference, yet they

ended up with a 6 seed in the Midwest. That year when our name was announced there was mild applause that was more polite than excited. As players,
we slumped in our chairs, dreading the seed and the site, trying desperately not
to show our true feelings.

This year, however, after a few minutes of yelling, high-fiving, and
hugging like WWF fans, we sat back in our seats pleasantly surprised.

After an entire year of feeling like we had been underrated, it finally felt
like we were given some respect. I don't remember much about who else went
where. We just all sat there amazed, that it was our name up on the screen next
to the No. 2 seed.

For the next half hour there was a lot of, "can you believe we got the No.
2 seed?" being asked.

After some celebrating we headed down to the locker room to discuss our
plans for practice, academics and travel for the upcoming week. Meanwhile
the crowd finished up the Selection Sunday show, waiting for us to re-emerge
to sign some autographs.

TOTAL SPORTS NETWORK

As we filed into the locker room, there were a few strangers in there with
cameras and boom microphones. We were told that ESPN was going to be
following us from that day on until we lost in the tournament. Apparently they
had done the same thing with Missouri the year before, every few days
showing the behind-the-scenes footage on ESPN's Sportscenter. I thought
maybe they were going to film a few meetings and practices, but soon realized
it was going to be an all-day, every day experience.

After concluding the meeting, we headed back up to the court where only
a few fans had left, and hundreds of kids lined up to get autographs. It felt

like a giant circus. While all the celebration was going on, KEZI was filming the Ernie Kent Coaches Show live from a corner of Mac Court. After signing a few autographs for kids that clearly wanted a Freddie Jones signature more than a Ben Lindquist, I took a seat on one of the bleachers and looked around at the unbelievable sight that was Mac Court.

I thought back over the year, even thinking back to the previous seasons, marveling at the state of Oregon basketball. We had been talking all year about this having the potential to be a magic ride, and as I sat there probably being a little too introspective, I realized that whatever happened that week in the tournament, the season had certainly been one of the greatest I'd ever experienced. Standing and shaking off the thoughts that were too deep for a celebration, I signed a few more autographs for kids who kept asking, "which one are you?" and headed home amazed at the day's events.

STUDENT-ATHLETES

With three days to prepare for an opponent we had never seen, we would be more than busy. In all the excitement, it only took an upcoming week of finals to remind us that we were student-athletes. In 1999 the first round took place right in the middle of finals, and the plan was to have some players take their finals when they got back, something that ended up backfiring and setting a few guys back.

This year Coach Kent wanted to try and get as many finals out of the way before finals week or during the tournament, but not after the scheduled times. When we met Monday, this was the first item he addressed. With finals still officially a week away, a number of projects and smaller assignments were due while we were out of town.

If we were to advance to the Sweet 16, the coaches wanted to make sure that we didn't have to worry about our finals the day of, or before our game.

The plan for the week was to have about four players take exams on the Friday between the first and second round games. Unfortunately I was one of those four.

THE GRIZZLIES

Montana made its way into the NCAA tournament and a No. 15 seed by winning the Big Sky Tournament, which they entered with a losing record and their coach's job in jeopardy. Before practice, our first tape of Montana had arrived. After going over their personnel we watched about 20 minutes of film.

At first glance they looked small and undermanned. But the more we watched, the more we realized that they were able to do some things really well. They had a few scorers, but mostly got along with tough defense and rebounding. It was clear that regardless of how good they really were, we were going to take them very serious and prepare just like we would for any other game.

Practice was spirited and went smoothly, even if it did feel a little awkward having two camera crews shuffling back and forth all around the court trying to get the right shot. Not much had changed with our team. However, the media attention had been altered dramatically. Before practice I went to get a few extra shots up, and thought maybe I was in the wrong gym when I walked through the door and found triple the reporters and cameras as usual. We hadn't even left Eugene and the media hype had already begun.

After practice one of the producers of the "all-access" ESPN gig asked if he and his crew could come over to my apartment and film me eating dinner. Hungry for a little TV time, who was I to get in the way of creative electronic journalism?

So that night the television people came over as Joy and I ate dinner. Assuming that they were going to get a few shots of me eating some chicken, or washing a dish, I was caught off guard when they sat and filmed our entire meal, at one point telling us, "just have a normal conversation."

Of course you can't just have a normal conversation with a camera and a giant microphone hanging over your head. When they finally walked out the door, I had wondered why I had said 'yes' to the whole thing. All though I was more curious who in America wanted to see me eat dinner, and a few days I found the answer to my question. Apparently nobody did. That segment ended up being part of the 20 hours of footage that had been left out of the four-minute piece two days later on Sportscenter.

After a routine practice the next day, we dressed in our coats and ties and met at the Casanova Center where the ESPN crew was already waiting, ready to make the trip. Because there wasn't a flight that went directly to Sacramento from Eugene, we were going to bus to Portland and catch a direct flight to Sacramento, and have a full day to get settled in before the game on Thursday afternoon.

MARCH MADNESS:

"Everyone is 0-0 when the tournament starts" — *Luke Jackson*

On the plane to Sacramento, one of the ESPN producers asked me if I wanted to go around the plane with a handicam and get some footage of everyone. They didn't take the Eugene camera crew on the plane with us, instead having another crew meet us at the airport in Sacramento. Since they still wanted to get some footage they brought the handicam for the plane ride.

Not having anything better to do, I agreed, taking the camera up the aisle and focusing the camera on each member of the team while adding my own personal commentary. When I finally arrived at Coach Kent's seat, he looked over and gave me the, "Ben, what are you doing" look. Then before I could come up with an excuse, he said, "Ben, what are you doing?"

This would not have been a big deal, but two years ago in the NCAA tournament, Kristian Christensen bought a video camera before the tournament to get footage. After a few days of doing mock interviews and filming just about everything, Coach Kent jokingly made a crack one day about Kristian filming, saying, "this wasn't a vacation." Without actually saying, "Kristian, put the camera away," indirectly that was exactly what he was saying to me.

So after a quick flash back to that experience, I calmly told him that the ESPN people had asked me to film a few of the guys. "Oh, I thought it was your camera" he said with a relieved smile, probably flashing back himself to the distraction at the last NCAA tournament.

As I was making my way from the front of the plane back to my seat, we encountered some turbulence, something I was never excited about.

Struggling down the narrow aisle of the plane like a drunken sailor, I continued my commentary, this time out of nervous energy. Assuming that once again the footage would be cut out of the next Sportscenter installment, I was surprised when they actually showed the camera shaking and me uneasily talking about the turbulence.

We arrived at our hotel in Sacramento well after 10 p.m. and immediately went to a small conference room where a buffet had been set up. It didn't take long to feed ourselves before Coach Kent told us to head right to bed and get some rest for the big day ahead of us.

THE MEDIA CIRCUS

The atmosphere of NCAA tournament is the closest thing to a media circus, with the exception of the Super Bowl. After practicing at the Sacramento Kings practice facility about 100 yards from Arco Arena, we lifted a few weights, and met in the locker room for our media session. Each day the team has to be available for an hour of media interviews in the locker room. This is where the team sits in the locker room, and, like kids waiting for Disneyland to open, the reporters hurry in to get interviews from certain players.

In addition to Coach Kent, three or four players go to a stage with microphones and rows of media in front. This is usually where you see all the interviews on TV after the games; ESPNEWS even broadcasts a few of the sessions live the day before the games. Because the reporters usually only interview the main players, this can become a boring time in the locker room. So guys usually walk up to a player who is getting interviewed on camera and try and get him to laugh in the middle of a serious comment. This almost always upsets the reporters who are diligently trying to get an interesting interview for the evening news.

After the media session, each team is given 45 minutes on the game floor to get used to shooting in the arena. Teams get their main practice at another site because the NCAA can't get eight teams on the same floor in one day without six teams getting either a really early time or a really late time. Most teams don't want to have practice at 6 p.m. the night before they play a game, nor do they want to have to get up and practice at 8 a.m., then sit around all day for a game the next night.

When we finally arrived back at the hotel, the exhaustion of practicing, sitting around, then practicing again had set in; everyone was ready to relax. After dinner we met briefly, skipping the walk-through and went to our rooms to get some rest.

The hotel we stayed in was one of the nicer ones of the year. When we showed up, I expected to be staying in the same hotels as the other seven tournament teams, but was surprised when I found out that the higher the team is seeded, the nicer the hotel it stays at. So because we had the highest seed, No. 2, we stayed at the nicest hotel. The other teams each stayed in a hotel decided by their seed, something that to no one's surprise upset USC, which was also playing in Sacramento.

The next day, when we arrived at Arco Arena before the game, there was a nervous buzz as we walked through the doors. When you first walk in the door, there is a booth set up to check you in and also check your bags for security purposes. When the support staff calls your name, you are handed a tournament pin that has the NCAA logo and the words "first round" on it. They hand you one of these for each game and practice session, distinguishing them with different colors for each day. From the moment you walk in the door, you get the feeling that you are really at the Big Dance!

In the locker room, we waited anxiously to get the o.k. to head onto the floor and get up some shots. The anxiety had begun to be unbearable. We were fortunate to get the second game of the day, but the wait still felt a day less than forever. The NCAA won't allow teams onto the floor until an hour before the game; even running a clock down to the exact time you can go on the floor. Tournament officials told us that even touching the ball could result in a penalty of some sort. I was curious to see what they would do if a player really did go out there and start shooting, but not curious enough to find out for myself.

Game time had finally arrived. After a season of going through the same routine every game, the only thing we wanted to hear was the sound of he horn signaling the start of the game. As coach talked about the game plan, each player was thinking about the game. A few of us had been to the tournament before, but we also had a lot of first-timers.

The energy and excitement of an NCAA tournament game is undeniable. Warm-ups were performed in front of a near sellout crowd that had finished watching Wake Forest defeat Pepperdine in the game before and was now eagerly waiting to see who Wake would play next.

The game began at an awkward pace; we looked more than just a step slow. Montana revealed its game plan early, making it clear that it wanted to keep us out of our usual fast-breaking pace. Each time we scored, missed, or even turned the ball over, the Grizzlies would walk the ball up the floor to try and control the speed of the game. The crowd, expecting to see the high flying Oregon team they had heard about, sat wondering if they were at the right game when we finally scored our 10th point halfway through the first half.

In a half where our offense was hiding, our defense at least kept us ahead, 10-8 with 10 minutes to play. The last 10 minutes of the half closely resembled the first; Montana was doing more than enough to keep ideas of an upset alive. In the final two minutes we were finally able to put together a few baskets and stretch the lead to 34-26.

During halftime Coach didn't talk about shooting the ball better or even defending better, instead he wanted us to relax and play our game. We had played solid defense, but in every other area we looked like the pressure of an entire season had finally gotten to us. We played the first half like a team up tight instead of the team that effortlessly flies up and down the floor. Through an entire season, we had been at the center of pressure-filled games going 16-0 at home and winning a PAC-10 championship not once flinching. Yet the unknown of the NCAA tournament had somehow tricked us into thinking the games were different.

In our usual huddle just outside the locker room, we talked about going out and playing like we knew we could play in the second half. We did just that initially, sprinting ahead 41-29. Montana responded and was able to stay in the game with its all-around fearless play, but with time running out we had begun to pull away. Even as a player, the last few minutes of the game had grown boring. The most exciting moment came in the final seconds as Freddie found himself all alone in the open court and finished with a thunderous dunk that gave us a 81-62 win and the school's first NCAA tournament win in 42 long years.

After shaking hands with the Montana players and gathering to say the Lord's Prayer we jogged unenthusiastically into the locker room. Although we had won the game, every player quietly sat dejected. As Coach Kent turned the corner that led into the locker room, he took a step back, surprised at what he saw.

"Let's not forget," he said, "we just won." As simple as it had sounded, he was right. As each player looked around the room, checking to make sure that it was o.k. to wipe the disappointed look off his face, we realized the most important thing, we were still playing. By the end of the first round the following day, 32 of the 64 teams would be on their way to spring break with their season over!

We, however, would be preparing for our tough second round opponent Wake Forest. We hadn't played our best game, but we had won, something that in the NCAA tournament is all that matters. Whether it was nerves, or just being out of sync, we knew that in order to defeat our second round opponent from the ACC we would have to play much better.

LOOSEN UP!

"You either stay alive or go home; our goal is to stay alive" — Anthony Lever

Before the first round you think about one thing, winning the first game. However, after getting the first win you begin to start thinking about a lot more. The next win now brings more than another opponent, and another city; it brings up ideas of something more. That something more is the Sweet 16, the tournament halfway mark, and the point where you can really start thinking about even bigger things like the Final Four.

With a match-up with the Demon Deacons of Wake Forest less than 48 hours away, our thoughts were no longer of the poorly played Montana game. We had our first taste of tournament action, and we wanted more. We knew we could play better and waiting two days to prove it seemed excruciating.

After showering back at the hotel, we headed to dinner. When we walked in the door there were several TV's showing the Trojans of USC, who were in the middle of a heated battle with the almost unheard of UNC-Wilmington. Fully expecting USC to be in control of the game, we were all shocked when the score flashed up and they were losing with only a few minutes to play.

We had been in the thick of March Madness, but, for some reason, watching the USC game finally gave us the feelings we had been accustomed to growing up. The excitement of a bigger team in the process of being upset by the underdog and as quickly as they had arrived being sent home by a close game was what we had remembered as we watched the tournament over the years.

Sitting in the noisy room, living and dying with each play, not sure who we wanted to win, things finally felt back to normal after our twilight-zone type game just hours earlier. The Montana game had felt like we were trying to cram the entire tournament into one game, not realizing that there were still three weeks left. But as we watched USC come back and send the game into overtime, we remembered what the tournament was all about, fun!

When the USC game went into overtime on a desperation three, we were sure the Trojans would wrap up the game and walk away, having avoided the upset bullet. However, 13th seeded UNC-Wilmington was not rattled, seemingly finding its second wind, making all the right play's down the stretch to win 93-89 in overtime.

For some reason we weren't as stunned after watching the game. USC had appeared ready to make a run deep into the tournament, but there the Trojans were, on their way home after just one game. Suddenly we remembered it wasn't so bad, and more importantly remembered we needed to loosen up and enjoy the experience.

With only a day to prepare for one of our toughest opponents of the year, it was back to work. After breakfast it was back to the books for a few of us. With a proctor monitoring and a camera crew over our shoulders, Anthony, Robert, Mark, team manager Greg Lawrence and I focused the best we could on our various exams. As soon as the tests were completed, it was off to the Arco Arena for a closed practice. Practice was not long. After getting some shooting in, we walked through Wake Forest's stuff and headed off to the mandatory media session.

Finally arriving back at the hotel after 4 p.m., the plan for the rest of the night was simple, eat, relax, and go to bed. After dinner and an early movie, Hud informed us of the now famous, "five-minute meeting." Walking into the room, knowing full well that there was no such thing as a "five-minute meeting," we sat down expecting to be there for at least the next half-hour.

"I'm not going to keep you here long," Coach said, which was greeted with rolled eyes and skeptical thoughts from the players. "This game is there for us to win. If we play our game, we will win."

After a couple of minutes Coach Kent wrapped it up, saying, "we'll see you in the morning."

Confused, we sat there expecting more, a walk-through, a quiz on their personnel, anything except a real "five-minute meeting."

"That's it?" I asked.

"That's it," he answered. Just like that we were done for the night.

Before heading to bed that night, I walked down to Rid's room to see how he was feeling about the game. The door to the room was propped open, so I knocked and walked in. When I opened the door, all the lights were off and the TV was on. Looking around to make sure it was the right room, I called Rid's name. Relieved I heard his half-awake voice, and asked if he was already heading to bed.

"Yep," he replied, "I'm pretty tired."

Flipping on the hall light, so that the situation wasn't completely awkward, I noticed on the wall a giant NCAA tournament bracket that had come from the local newspaper and had been taped to the wall with athletic tape. All the first round winners had been updated; leaving the rest to be added after each round. However, upon closer inspection I found the word OREGON had been filled in from the bottom right corner of the bracket all the way to the championship game.

Without commenting on the confidently filled in bracket, I sat in a chair by the bed. As usual I asked, "What's up?"

"I think if we play the way we can, we'll win" he responded, knowing exactly what I was asking. After a few minutes of small talk, I got up and said, "I just wanted to come down here and tell you that I have a feeling you're going to play great tomorrow." Without saying much else, I walked out the door, not thinking about what I had said, but instead about what he had written.

I had gone down there to give him a little confidence boost before a big game, and somehow I was the one walking out of there feeling good about the game tomorrow. Not from anything I had said, but instead by the simple tournament bracket on the wall. I felt confident that if nothing else, the ball was going to be in the hands of a guy who was ready to play.

The next day we walked through their plays after breakfast instead of going to the arena for a shoot-around. With an early afternoon tip-off, getting rested and focused was more important than the trouble it took to get to and from the arena. We knew that it was going to be a physical game, Wake Forest, played typical East Coast basketball, relying on a physical inside presence and tough defense. They had played all four of the No. 1 seeded teams in the tournament, and had battled through the always difficult ACC. There was no hiding the fact that it was going to take our best effort to win the game and advance to the Sweet 16.

THE SCREEN

The game started with bang, literally. With less than a minute gone, big Chris set a high screen for Rid to come off and make a play. Wake guard Broderick Hicks was defending Rid when he was crushed by Chris's monster screen. Hicks was sent to the ground dazed and bloodied. Chris, meanwhile, stood there wondering if he should help the guy up or roll unguarded to the basket. Hicks went to the bench with a bloodied lip and a headache. During the next timeout, Chris came over to the bench and yelled excitedly, "That's an ACC screen." The talk had been about how physical Wake Forest played, however, with 39 minutes left Chris had set the tone early, not by a blocked shot or thunderous dunk, but with a screen.

The first half was every bit exciting as the sellout crowd had expected. Both teams were taking their best shot and neither was backing down. We had expected a hard-fought game, and we were getting even more than that. With the exception of a few baskets by Chris, the majority of our points were coming from the rock-solid play of Freddie, Luke and Rid. For a team that relied on the solid play of every player, this type of lopsided scoring was a concern at halftime. After trailing early Wake had come back and taken control of the game to lead 48-46 at the half.

"We're right there, guys," Luke Jackson said in the locker room at halftime. We had shaken off the tight play of our first game, and, at the halfway point, we found ourselves in the middle of what felt like another PAC-10 game. As usual Coach Kent settled us down and made defensive adjustments on Craig Dawson, who was shooting the lights out; and Antwan Scottand, who along with Darius Songalia, had been scoring on the inside.

"You can be tired in April, but right now you've got to do whatever it takes and find a way to win" Coach said.

In the first minute of the second half we were able to tie the game at 48-all, but that seemed to hurt more than it helped. Wake Forest scored eight straight points and had put an end to any momentum we tried to get coming out of the locker room. The next 10 minutes was spent trying to get something going. Every time we narrowed the lead, Wake answered with another run. The game had started to feel like it was slipping. It was one of those games where you feel like you can't get over the hump but, if you could, you'd win.

The big three of Freddie, Luke, and Rid had been the only ones to score since Chris's dunk early in the first half, and this pattern felt like it was going to cost us. We were finally able to get the lead down to one point, and had the crowd back in the game, until Wake was able to get a rare four-point play that took the wind out of our sails.

On our next play Freddie and Craig Dawson, who had continued his hot shooting, became tangled on an offensive rebound. On a bizarre play, Dawson let out a scream of pain as he came out of the tangle holding his shooting arm. Without paying any attention, Freddie grabbed the rebound, looked around and found a wide-open and wide-eyed Jackson right in front of our bench.

As Jackson set up as he had so many times before for his smooth left-handed stroke, my heart stopped. The pressure was getting to me and I was on the bench. Sitting directly behind him, I could see the entire flight of the ball. As soon as it left his hand, I knew it was in although it took the ball softly falling through the net for me to believe it. The crowd had awakened like a sleeping giant as we cut the deficit back to two. Somehow the shot had awakened more than the crowd.

Wake Forest called a timeout to get the injured Dawson to the bench. He was later diagnosed with a dislocated shoulder. With Dawson out of the game, it felt like Wake's threat from the outside was gone.

On the next play we got a defensive stop. Rid then threw the ball up the right side of the floor to Luke Jackson and, just as smoothly as the time before, he hoisted a potentially devastating three. The shot looked a little off and, as Wake Forest was waiting to catch the rebound and head the other way, Freddie came from the weak side, caught the ball as it perfectly bounced off the rim and threw down a game-changing, two-handed dunk!

The crowd erupted out of surprise and excitement. Out of all the spectacular dunks in Freddie's four-year career, this one came at a point in the game where we needed a basket the most, the right bounce, the right player and the right place combined to change the entire game. With the dunk the score was tied, and Wake Forest was on its heels. After another defensive stop, two Rid free throws gave us the first lead since midway through the first half.

Wake battled back with the inside play of Songalia, but the momentum had already changed. With three minutes remaining, Rid came down the floor like he had done all year and fired in his seventh three-pointer of the game, finally breaking the Demon Deacons.

The final minutes were heart-pounding as Wake made one last charge. The clutch foul shooting of Luke Jackson in the final minute wrapped up a 10-for-10 day at the line with the last one tying his career high of 29 points.

With only 17 seconds remaining and a four-point lead, Robert Johnson put in a free throw that gave us a 90-85 lead. It was, unbelievably, the first point by a player other than Freddie, Luke, and Rid in just under 34 minutes.

After a few harmless three-point attempts, the horn sounded, giving us a 92-87 win and our first trip to the Sweet 16 since 1960. Amazingly, out of those 92 points the big three had scored 81 — Freddie with 24, Rid with 28, and Jackson with his 29.

Since Chris's basket in the first half, they had been on a three- man 71-point run.

The whole game I sat there wondering if they could keep up the way they were scoring, and even when I read the box score after the game, it was hard to conceive three guys accounting for almost 90 percent of a team's scoring. The only thing more amazing than the individual performances of the big three was the come-from-behind victory that looked like certain defeat.

"Just like we've done all-year, we found a way to win!" Coach said in the locker room after the game.

After a couple of minutes of celebration, everyone just sat there, trying to take it all in before the media stormed the locker room. We had done it all year. Whether it was our blistering shooting, or our timely defense, we had found a way to win. The best part of the win was looking around the room, every guy was happy, not just for himself, but for his teammates. We had believed in each other and stuck behind each other the entire year.

"Wake had something to prove; they played their best game, and went beyond testing us, but once again we hung in there like we did all year," Anthony reflected.

An hour-and-a-half after the game, the feeling of going to the Sweet 16 still hadn't set in as we bused back to the hotel. The magical season that had been so often referred to throughout the year was finally starting to appear. For the first time we had all started to realize that we were in the midst of more than something special. This was something that would take months to realize its full magnitude.

"There was something different in the air, I didn't exactly know what, but it just felt like we had done something special, but weren't able to fully experience it yet," Rid later said.

After the game we headed back to the hotel where Hud told us that we would be chartering back to Eugene instead of flying on a commercial plane. The trip kept getting better, after a big win, we liked the idea of having a plane to ourselves at our convenience. So, after eating and packing up, we met in the lobby as we waited for the coaches and administrators to join us. When we pulled up to a private airfield, I realized that we weren't going to be taking just any chartered airplane. I had heard stories of the football team chartering an entire commercial airline for its games, and thought maybe we might be doing the same thing, just on a smaller plane.

When the bus pulled 30 feet from the plane, we started to feel like rock stars jetting from one tour site to the next. When I looked out the window and saw the Boeing 727 without any commercial airline markings, I began to realize that this wasn't any ordinary charter. When we boarded the plane, the first portion looked like the fancy first class on any other plane, which I assumed, was going to the coaches and administrators.

However, as I made my way to the back of the plane I realized that it got even better. Each seat looked like a leather Lazy Boy, and for traditionally cramped basketball players, this was more than satisfactory.

After a smooth take-off that made a luxury sedan feel bumpy, I asked the stewardess who had flown on the plane before. Her unenthusiastic response, "Oh, well we took U2 on one of their tours for six months," and, as if I wasn't impressed yet, she continued, "the President of Mexico, Keanu Reeves, and Christina Aguelara, but that's just in the last year or so."

Sitting in the fully reclining Lazy Boy-like seat, I felt like I was dreaming. In one short year we had gone from a struggling self-destructing team that watched the tournament from home to a championship team that was in the thick of an NCAA tournament run, and flying on a rock star's plane. If life got much better for a college basketball player, I'd like to see it. For us, it felt great to be a DUCK!

It was hard to believe that in one weekend 64 teams had been reduced to only 16. It's humbling to think that you play an entire season to try and be one of the 64, yet the season-long wait can be over after one game.

On the plane, I sat talking to Anthony, Greg, and our assistant trainer Tina, "This would make a great book," I half jokingly said. I had always thought it would be fun to write a book, but had no idea what to write about. As I sat there I realized that this was as great an opportunity as any. It felt like more than just a success story that had resulted in a championship and national recognition. There was so much that went into getting us where we were. And as we thought back over some of the great stories of the year, it became apparent that this year would be special not because of the many accomplishments of our team, but instead because of the special team that accomplished so much.

THE ARRIVAL

When we touched down in Eugene, the excitement and energy that had been bubbling over had turned to exhaustion and fatigue. When we stepped off the plane at the private gate, we heard cheering. Then, as we neared the fence that led to the waiting bus, we saw a group of about 150 people who had once again braved the cold to greet us at the airport. As we made our way towards them, the fatigue quickly turned back to excitement as they became even louder. Forming a tunnel that was about 30 yards long, we high-fived and signed autographs for the excited fans who had been waiting patiently for our arrival.

Along with the fans, there were a few TV reporters who conducted interviews. After about 30 minutes of commotion, we finally boarded the bus and headed for the Casanova Center where twice as many fans waited. It had been a big deal for our team to be heading to the Sweet 16, but when we pulled up we realized how important it was for the community, too. Many of the fans had lived the season almost as much as we had, and it felt good to reward them with something special.

Chris's solid presence in the low post, a major factor in our success!

CHAPTER 11
How Sweet 16 It Is!

*"Confidence is preparation, everything else
is beyond your control" — Richard Kline*

Although we believed we could get to the second week of the NCAA
tournament, it seemed like a strange position to be in for a team that became a
disappointment just a season ago. This was a new experience to every player
on the team. A few of us had been to the tournament and every one of us
had experienced forms of success on the basketball court. Still, somehow part
of the success we were experiencing was a result of the fact that no one had
been where we were going. Two things happen when a player or a team is in a
position it has never been in. One, they get nervous because of the unfamiliar
situation and perform stiff and tight, assuming that because nobody thought
they could be there they shouldn't. The second thing that happens is because
they have never been in that particular position they don't place limitations or
boundaries on what they can accomplish and play with nothing to lose.

Playing with nothing to lose was exactly what we were doing. Nobody
knew who this team from Oregon was, and kept waiting the entire year for our
wild ride to come to an abrupt stop so they could say, "we knew it wouldn't
last."

Getting a team not to think about the magnitude of the games it is playing
is difficult. However, collectively our team seemed to be doing it through
osmosis. It didn't seem real that we were quickly moving up the list of the
greatest teams in Oregon history and putting our program on the map not as a

one-year wonder, but the team and style that players and coaches around the country wanted to duplicate.

That morning when I woke up, it was impossible not to be in an excited and reflective mood. Watching our clips from the Wake Forest game the night before was a stark contrast from the brief score that flashed up after the UMASS loss earlier in the year. Back when player's names were mispronounced and anchor Linda Cohn referred to our team as the struggling Ducks led by Ernie Kent. Now the word was spreading, we were for real, and Duck fans were popping up all over the country.

The day after our victory over Wake Forest, we were still waiting to find out who our opponent would be. We had finished up the second round on a Saturday and the next day all gathered at various places to watch the game between Mississippi State and Texas where the Longhorns came back and won. In a meeting that afternoon, we gathered to find out the details of the upcoming road trip. There was an unfamiliar excitement in the air. It wasn't hard to realize that we didn't want this ride to end; a drastic change from a year ago when some players and coaches would have been fine with the season ending a month early.

It was announced we would be leaving Wednesday for Madison, Wisconsin, and playing the longhorns two days later on Friday. By Monday we had game tape and an extensive scouting report, but when it came to preparation we did what had gotten us there, focused on ourselves. At this point in the year you fall into a routine and the preparation becomes like clockwork. You watch game tape, study the scouting report, and then walk through their plays. With a PAC-10 championship in hand and a trip to the Sweet 16 on the table, there was no reason to reinvent the wheel.

Things ran somewhat smoothly over the next two days. Practice was intense and everyone's outlook was positive. With the academic term racing to the finish line, there was no time to relax and think about anything but preparing for the game and our exams. Myself, Rid, Mark and team managers Greg and Tom were all a part of a group Internet project that involved creating a Website about some form of art. We had arrived back in Eugene Saturday night and the project was due Monday night. After procrastinating, we had started to wonder how on earth we were supposed to create a Website in two days while at the same time preparing for another one of the biggest games of the year.

The next day was a scramble, Coach Kent moved practice around so that we could get the project finished, and we all ended up sitting in the computer lab attempting to come up with something halfway decent. After about six hours of staring at a computer screen, we had put together a Website that included links to each person's golf course of choice. By the end of the thing we had created a quality project, and as we were finishing up the ESPN cameras came in and filmed some shots of the finished project. Exhausted we took a few hours off, and then went back to practice.

The next two days flew by. Before we knew it, Wednesday had arrived. That morning we were on our way to the airport to board another chartered plane. However, this time the charter was taking more people and therefore the school had chartered a commercial plane instead of the fancy plane from the week before. Although the last plane was a taste of lifestyles of the rich and famous, as long as we were able to stretch our feet across a few seats, we were all happy.

When the plane touched down in Madison, we were greeted by charter buses and taken to our hotel. We were given about an hour and then it was off to practice at some Division III school gym that made my high school gym look big. The purpose of this practice was more to get the flight and long bus rides out of our systems as opposed to a real organized and extensive practice. Within two hours of arriving at the gym we were on our way back to the hotel to relax and get some rest.

As we entered the hotel I had flashbacks of a Las Vegas casino. Apparently there was a huge pool tournament going on in the hotel and the smoking that seems to be synonymous with bars and pool tables had spilled over into our hotel. This would have been fine in a regular hotel, but this particular one was a 10-story building with a giant atrium-like inside that was open. The result, by the end of the night the top two levels of the hotel looked like a smog-filled day in L.A.. This might not have been so bad, but we were all on top floor of the hotel where the smog made its home.

When we woke up the next morning, we all seemed to feel like we had rolled 20 years of smoking into one night. That morning at breakfast there were a number of complaints about the smoke and also the noise that 300 beer-drinking pool players can make. Deciding that there wasn't much we could do about the whole situation, we made our complaints and dropped the subject.

Around noon we made our way to the tournament site for practice at the Kohl Center, home of the Wisconsin Badgers. The magnitude of the game set in as Kansas was exiting the floor, and we ended up practicing in front of a few thousand fans that were customarily let in to the practice sessions the day before tournament games. Practice was about an hour long and consisted of fast break drills, a lot of shooting and simply getting a feel for the arena. Coach Kent was always on the idea of getting a feel for the gym. In fact, often times we would spend more time shooting than preparation because of the importance our shooting played in our style of play.

MEDIA CIRCUS

Just as the level of competition was raised in the second week of the NCAA tourney, so to was the media hype. The gamble of picking one team to follow through the tournament was paying off for ESPN. We were informed that our segment on Sportscenter was the highest rated portion of the show.

ESPN wasn't the only one that took part in the media frenzy called March Madness. There was so much media attention each day leading up to the games that you would have thought the players and coaches being interviewed were announcing world peace instead of game plans and their thoughts about a game. The media circus had continued and, for a team trying to get on the map of big time college basketball, it was well worth it.

After practice we spent an hour and half in the locker room with the media doing interviews, regularly pulling Rid, Fred, Jackson, and Coach Kent to do interviews on the main podium where most of the post game interview clips are shown on Sportscenter. For doing so little that day, we were ready to get back to the hotel. From the observations I was making, part of being successful in the tournament was just as much managing the schedule and distractions as it was about X's and O's. As ridiculous as it sounds, sitting around answering the same questions for an hour and a half, then practicing can be as grueling as an overtime game.

Back at the hotel it was time to relax and head to dinner. After a nap and a regular dose of television, our young bodies had recovered just in time for the evening's walk-through. We were greeted by the camera and mics of the ESPN crew who we had finally started to adjust to. By this time we no longer felt like the tournament's reality TV show. Once everyone was seated, Coach Kent got right to the point. "This is a game we should win," he said. "We have talked all year about getting to the Final Four. This is the next step."

When the meeting concluded, we teamed it up as usual and headed back through the lobby where the noise from the delirious pool players had begun. In our rooms the cardboard-like doors were no match for the 40-year-old drunk bachelors yelling pick-up lines from one floor to another. With the entire inside of the hotel open space from the first to the tenth floor, it had begun to get loud and what had seemed like a calm relaxing environment quickly turned to steady noise.

I was watching TV when a frustrated Anthony got up, grabbed a towel out of the bathroom, rolled it up, pressed it along the space between the door, then, without saying a word, sat back down. Until that point the door had been no match for the noise and the smoke. I thought the towel under the door thing was amusing, and couldn't help but glance over with a smile, choosing to hold back on any smart remark I was easily conjuring up.

Although the noise had awakened a few people, for the most part sleep was not hard to come by after a long couple of days. As usual the phone rang signaling it was time to wake up. After a few minutes team manager Greg Lawrence made his routine follow-up call, informing us of when and where breakfast would be. Game day had arrived, and so had the focus that had become common the last month and a half. With the earlier game, we were on a tight schedule. After breakfast and the occasional Coach Kent comment, we went to the arena for our regular game-day shoot-around. Keeping things short and sweet we broke a light sweat and were off the floor in 40 minutes.

HOOK 'EM HORNS

Coming down the glass elevators from the tenth floor of the hotel you could see a number of people gathered in the lobby. As the elevator descended, the noise of musical instruments grew louder. On the ride down I had just hoped that whatever was making all the noise wouldn't be there when we got back to the hotel that night.

When the doors opened we quickly discovered the source. The school band and cheerleaders had formed two lines leading out the door to the bus, serenading us to the school fight song. My frustration with the noise was instantly turned to school pride as we strolled to the bus, wondering what other school did something this unique.

As we boarded the bus and began to make our way out of the hotel parking lot, police cars pulled in front and behind the bus, giving us an official escort during the 20-minute drive to the arena. Although it wasn't quite presidential, they did manage to turn their lights on and wave us through a few red lights.

As I sat in the back of the bus it was hard not to think that perhaps this could be the end of my college basketball career. I sat hoping that somehow this wouldn't be the end. To me it didn't seem like the right way to end such a great season although I realized Gonzaga was probably saying the same thing after a disappointing first round loss that ended its great run the week before.

The short trip to the locker room was made with anxious steps. We couldn't wait to step onto the court. After getting settled in the locker room players started to trickle out onto the floor. Fans had already begun to arrive, and Duck fans that had made the long trip cheered as we jogged out and started stretching. The hour until game time felt unbearable. You can only do so much stretching, and we didn't want to get too many shots up for the fear of using energy prematurely.

In the locker room silence prevailed. Each player sat quietly in his own little world. Robert Johnson's head was covered with a towel as if to block out any distractions. Each player did his own little thing before the game. Some listened to music; others put their head in their hands. Regardless of what or how, we were all doing the same thing, just differently. There is something reassuring to a player when you can take a few minutes to calm yourself down whether from nerves or excitement. You feel a little helpless before a game you have waited and prepared for because you're stuck in a locker room to sort through the numerous scenarios that will present themselves throughout the game.

The pre-game talk is usually a hybrid of every meeting and comment made throughout the week leading up to the game. Coach Kent sensed our restlessness and kept his remarks brief, covering the game plan and plugging as much confidence into the game as he could. We felt ready and, as I surveyed the room, I was reassured by the looks on everyone's faces.

WE AIN'T GOING NO WHERE !

Forming a huddle outside the locker room, we began our regular chant started by, " We ain't going no where." The fans above us in the stands seemed amused and intrigued by our unusual chant. As we finished up and ran onto the floor our confidence and humility, which throughout the year had been rolled into a team, drew cheers from our newfound fans who seemed re-freshed by our obvious passion for the game.

Texas made its entrance and received some cheers from Longhorn fans, but the Duck faithful made a special effort to make them feel unwelcome by the use of the BOO! The Longhorns were a skilled team that played in the tough Big 12 that was loaded with teams like eventual Final Four teams Kansas and Oklahoma. They were led by freshman guard T. J. Ford, who was the first freshman to ever lead the country in assists. They had a balanced team that had lost a starter to a knee injury earlier in the year, forcing them to find different ways to win games. Although we had film and a decent paper trail on them, it's still difficult to feel totally prepared when you are used to seeing each team twice a year in conference play. As they warmed up they looked big, quick and confident, a combination you love to have as a team, but don't really care to face in an opponent.

This was college basketball — a packed arena, loud fans, two quality teams facing off with only one moving on. It didn't take a basketball purist to appreciate the setting, but if you were a purist, this was what the game is all about. The arena was packed and, as the game was about to begin, each team's starters were introduced. After that we huddled up and all together yelled, "Dominate."

The game got off to a clumsy start, Texas was visibly nervous and the Longhorns' play proved it. We didn't look nervous but instead over-excited to play. However, it only took a few errant passes and poor shot selection by Texas to help us realize the game was ours for the taking. Basket after basket we began to roll. The game was slipping away from Texas and the 'Horns knew it. They had opened the game 0-6 and would go on to commit 12 first half turnovers. Just as soon as I started to think that this was too easy, and we might end up beating them by 25, they went on a run. With two minutes left in the first half our lead was only five points, 33-28.

Then, almost as though he was upset that they had gotten back into the game, Rid broke free for a 3-pointer that started an 8-0 run. L. Jackson put the finishing touches on with it a 3-pointer just before the buzzer. With the momentum back in our hands we headed to the locker room with a 41-28 lead. We had played a solid first half, featuring a balanced team with continuing great play from the Luke's. There had been one surprise, however. Through 20 minutes our leading scorer, Freddie, only had two points.

Taking his position in front of the chalk board Coach Kent began, "We're right were we want to be, but they are going to make another run." That was something they had done in their last game against Mississippi State. Texas had showed signs of fatigue, and part of talk at halftime was to continue the up-and-down pace that had helped us get our 13-point first half lead. Although Freddie had struggled to get going offensively, his defense had still been a huge factor in the game. In the back of my mind it was hard not to wonder what impact another half like the first from our leading scorer would have on the outcome of the game.

We expected Texas to get back into the game, and the first 10 minutes of the second half the Horns did just that. After trading baskets we still had our 13-point lead and control of the game, 51-38. However, Texas used a blistering 13-0 run to tie the game at 51-51 with a little over 11 minutes to play. We had our chance to control the game, but open threes and easy baskets had let Texas back in the game and the control up in the air. The next 10 minutes featured classic tournament basketball full of play making, tough defense, and impressive outside shooting. Luke and Luke were shining again, while Robert had continued his defense while adding timely scoring. Freddie, however, looked out of sync on offense, never quite finding his stroke.

With the clock beginning to run dry and Texas more than in the game, the future began to look cloudy. With our style of back-and-forth play, the game could easily come down to a lucky bounce or a questionable call, all things you hate to lose a game on.

With a minute to play, we held an uncomfortable two-point lead. Texas forward James Thomas had come alive in the second half and, with 23 seconds left, received the ball in the post, made an aggressive move and scored a short basket. As the ball was leaving his hands, the whistle blew. The ref gave the dramatic tomahawk, count-the-basket motion, signaling that the basket was good and he would be shooting a foul shot.

Everyone looked up and down the bench trying to recall whether or not Thomas was a good free throw shooter. A few "60 and 65 percents" were thrown around, but with the game virtually on the line, anything was possible. As much as I wanted to believe that we were still going to win, it had appeared as though we had shot ourselves in the foot one too many times.

As Thomas trotted to the foul line, his teammates were trying to provide as much confidence as possible. The ref tossed him the ball at the line; he took a few dribbles, then gently gathered himself and released the ball.

"Please miss," I repeated in my head over and over.

Approaching the rim at what looked like too great a speed, the ball careened off the side and into Robert Johnson's hands. The entire bench took a deep breath. With the game tied 70-70, we still had a chance to win.

The situation was more than familiar. Our last two games of the conference season had come down to last-second baskets, and this to was eerily similar. With the ball in hand Freddie slid across the half-court line, knowing full well that, with the score tied and only 23 seconds on the clock, we needed the last shot of the game.

Although Rid and Jackson had carried the offensive load for the majority of the game, there was no question who would be taking the final shot, Freddie! With two game-winning shots, including the Pac-10 championship-sealing basket under his belt, there was no question that if someone were going to take a shot with the game on the line it would be Freddie.

With the clock continuing to wind down, Freddie stood 40 feet from the basket as all 10 players and the thousands in attendance sat watching, waiting for either the conclusion to a great game or the continuation to overtime. As players from both teams began to take their position for what was to come, things moved in slow motion. Freddie held the ball on his hip; looked up as the clock clicked just on top of 10 seconds, assessing the situation one more time. He put the ball on the floor and made his move from the left corner just past the halfcourt line towards the top of the key. Could he honestly deliver again, or was it to good to be true?

With the Texas defender playing directly in front of him, Freddie was quickly approaching the three-point line and building momentum. You could tell right away that the defender was tentative and unsure of how he was going to guard Freddie. Before the Texas player could make up his mind, Freddie had made his move and had already gone past him. Not wanting to foul and already beaten on the drive, the defender was caught in no man's land, and therefore out of the play. As the next defender in the Texas line of defense,

Deginald Erskin rotated from the weak side, stepping up between Freddie and the hoop. Where other players might have rushed a shot or panicked, Freddie did neither. Gathering himself and with both feet he took a giant leap more important than any of the thunderous dunks in his four-year career. As he floated through the air the defender slid underneath him with the idea of taking a charge on the play. Adapting immediately, Freddie shifted his body in mid-air and, by doing so, turned the tables on the defender, forcing him to back off of his original plan of taking a charge.

As Freddie reached the pinnacle of his jump, he took the ball in his outstretched right arm and began the initial stages of the finger roll. Almost as though some one had hit the switch on the VCR remote, sending the game out of slow motion and back to the fast pace at which it had been played, the ball seemed to leap out of his hand and softly brushed the back of the rim on its way through the hoop.

Confused and surprised, the Longhorns quickly called a timeout to set up a final play with 2.8 seconds showing on the clock. They had to travel the length of the floor and only had 2.8 seconds to do so. Our plan was to contain the drive and not foul, which would hopefully force them into a poor desperation shot. However, the NCAA tournament is famous for unbelievable plays where desperate prayers are answered. So with a two-point lead, 90 feet and 2.8 seconds, there was still no room for error.

We had figured Texas would get the ball to speedy guard T. J. Ford with the intention of having him fly down the floor and making a play. When the ball was in-bounded they did just that, running a few screens to get him the ball as close to halfcourt as possible. In a game where the last 20 seconds seemed to be minutes, the last 2.8 seconds went like lightning. As Ford caught the ball, he had crossed the halfcourt line before the clock had even reached 2.0, he was headed down the right sideline and was getting dangerously close to the three-point line. With the time running down, he gathered himself on the run and put up a running jump shot that looked right on line. However, as the horn sounded the ball grazed the backboard and rim as a Texas player rebounded it too late. In denial he tried to lay the ball in hoping that the clock hadn't run dry. But the final score was Oregon 72, Texas 70.

The last minute had been an emotional roller coaster, but that seemed to be quickly forgotten as we shook hands before waiting to celebrate our improbable trip to the Elite 8. Along with the brilliant performances of Jackson and Rid, who finished with a combined 45 points, it had essentially been another all-around team win where it took a big contribution from every player on the floor to get the win. Chris and Robert were rock-solid in the post, while Anthony and James were dependable off the bench, and even Mark Michaelis had provided a few surprising baskets. Most important of all though, was the final play of Freddie Jones who regardless of a 2-for-6, four-point performance never lost the confidence that had made him our best player and team leader. He had provided another memorable and spectacular moment that had done more than win us another basketball game.

ONE STEP CLOSER

In the locker room there was plenty of excitement, in a tournament where the goal is to move on one game at a time, we had done just that. As Coach Kent strolled in, positioning himself in the front of the room he stood quiet, processing the game, trying to get a handle on the magnitude of the win and the chance to be play our next game with a chance to go to the Final Four. "You've done more than prove you've earned the No. 2 seed in the tournament," he began, " but this is not over, this team is good enough to get to the Final Four."

With a game against the winner of the game between Kansas and Illinois, only a day and a half away, rest was more important than ever. After the game Luke and Luke sat slumped over in their chairs too exhausted to do anything else. Looking at their faces, it was clear the game had taken its toll on them physically and mentally. After changing and gathering our stuff, we headed out into the stands to catch the first half of the Kansas-Illinois game. The night was still young and we would be getting dinner and meeting that night to discuss our next game plan.

Kansas controlled the first half and although the Jayhawks hadn't pulled away yet, it seemed likely that they would be our next opponent. After dinner we met back in the ballroom where the excitement of the big win had now turned into shear exhaustion. Around 11 p.m. that night the meeting began, and, in about 20 minutes it was over. After giving us an overview of each Kansas player and a few other important scouting tips, we were excused with simple instructions, "Go to Bed."

About midnight the simple instructions about going to bed, became more complex. The pool players were intent on outdoing themselves from the night before. As exhausted as we were, it was like trying to sleep under the stage of a rock concert, and at 2 a.m. their yelling and arguing woke about half the team up from what sleep they had managed. A few of us poked our heads out to see what was going on below. We saw a number of drunken pool players yelling at each other.

The next morning at breakfast, it was clear that another night in the hotel wasn't going to work. That morning we were told to pack our bags because there might be a possibility we could switch to another hotel. Around noon we headed to the arena for practice and a media session. Practice was light and relaxed. Even Nike CEO Phil Knight attended. With only a day between games, it made no sense to do more than walk through Kansas's plays and shoot around.

After practice it was back to the locker room for the next media session. This time we were required to wait in the locker room while our media guy

Greg Walker would come and get the people they wanted to interview outside in the designated area. To sum up the situation we ended up sitting in the locker room with nothing to do. Realizing this might happen I decided to bring a few decks of cards in the hopes that we could get a chance to play a few hands. Within 15 minutes we had 10 guys around a table playing what was supposed to be blackjack, but with a few of our own rules. Even though there was no money on the line, we were still dealing with competitive athletes, so when someone lost a hand it wasn't all smiles, and when someone won, there was a little trash talking. The number of people on the table continued to grow until there were no more chairs, and as someone was called into an interview, there was someone there to take his place.

We were together. It was different and it was fun, and it was exactly what our team was all about. The ability of 15 guys from all over the country and even parts of the world to come together had been the story of the season. It didn't seem to matter if it was floating down a river, revealing our deepest fears, pulling together to win a championship that was slipping away, or playing cards in a locker room like we had grown up together. Whatever it was, we had done it together!

We had packed up our stuff before practice with the possibility of changing hotels. On our way out of the arena parking lot the possibility became reality. We took a short drive and found ourselves at the edge of a lake and in front of a hotel appropriately called The Edgewater. As we walked through the doors, we wondered why we hadn't stay there in the first place. Then, as we looked around we knew why. Texas signs dotted the lobby of the hotel. The Longhorns had been the previous guests until we had beaten them the day before.

After we had settled in, we had about an hour before we headed to dinner. Curious and tired of being cooped up, about eight of us decided to go outside. On the lake side of the hotel was a walking path and a deck that in the summer was probably used a great deal. But, towards the end of winter all it offered was a view of a frozen Lake.

After a few minutes of looking out over the lake, Brian Helquist, the team's strong man, picked up one of the giant rocks that lined the lake, put it on his shoulder and tossed it as far as he could. As the rock crashed down on the icy surface, we all expected it to disappear into the water underneath. However, the rock simply bounced a few times and stopped, sitting on the surface without so much as a dent in the ice. This not only got all of our attention, but also tempted us to join the cause. Brian, upset and also surprised, was reloading, this time with a bigger rock and a serious look, determined to break through the ice.

After everyone had taken a few shots at cracking the surface, we childishly dared someone to walk out onto the ice. James was the smallest and lightest and, without much debate, slowly walked onto the ice. Slowly more of us followed, as we continued picking up the rocks we had already thrown, trying to get them farther and farther out.

By this time you could see other guests in their rooms looking out their windows, trying to figure out what the heck we were doing. Just then one of the coaches came out and ordered us off the ice, reminding us that we were playing for a chance to go to the Final Four the next day. As we carefully walked off the ice, it was apparent how ridiculous the whole idea was, but, with smiles on our faces, it was definitely one of the highlights of the trip.

Walk-through that night was serious and intense; things had begun to tighten up and we could all feel it. Afterwards, on our way out of the ballroom, we decided to have a players only meeting to make sure we are all on the same page. Down in Rid's room we all made ourselves comfortable. After a few jokes about the smell of the room, we waited for someone to begin the meeting. Our team meetings were an interesting process. Usually we would joke around for a few minutes and then sit silently waiting to see who would start. That's when Freddie and Rid would look at each other trying to get the other to begin. One or the other would finally say a few things about the game. Then everyone else would add his two cents. This seemed to happen in every players-only meeting we had.

"Fellas, we can win this game; we've come too far not to," Freddie said after a three-minute friendly stand-off over who would start the meeting. Then Rid said a few things about believing we could win, and the floodgates had opened.

"They think we're scared to play them" one person chimed in, " If we play our game, no one can play with us" someone else added. This continued for 10 minutes, and like a session of therapy everyone felt relaxed and focused again, kind of like when you've had a bad day and you need to get something off your chest. This short meeting served as our way of getting every nervous, anxious, or uncertain feeling out of our systems, even if it was only for a night. After all, on game day those feelings can only be cured by one thing, the opening tip.

Freddie doing what he does...the Unbelievable

CHAPTER 12
A Shot at the Best of the Best

"Shoot for the moon. Even if you miss,
you'll land among the stars" — Les Brown

The morning of the game at breakfast I sat looking out over the frozen lake thinking back over the year. I thought of all the memorable moments that had made the year so special. Many were about basketball, but equally represented was the time spent off the court with the guys. While playing with the bacon on my plate I started to listen to Coach Kent covering the schedule for the rest of the day. The day was to be as routine as usual; with the one exception... we were playing in the Elite 8!

The bus ride to the arena was silent; at some point or another the fact that a win would place us amongst the best of the best crossed every player's mind. You'd have to have the mind of Buddha to block out the magnitude of this game.

Kansas posed a number of problems. The Jayhawks were faster and more skilled in the frontcourt, well-coached, and had guards who could flat-out play the game. I felt confident that we could control the guard portion, but with NBA lottery picks at the center and power forward, they certainly had the advantage on paper. Kansas had spent a good part of the year ranked No. 1 in the country, and was an easy pick for the regional No. 1 seed by the selection committee. It was no secret that a win would require our best game of the year, but we were confident they, too, would need their best.

As both teams stretched and warmed-up, CBS announcers Bill Raftery and Verne Lundquist were on the court getting a good look at both teams. The crowd had already filed in and was cheering. It felt like a scene right out the championship game from Hoosiers. With the pre-game clock winding down, we descended back into the locker room one last time.

Coach Kent looked around and then began, "Sometimes I have to sit back and look…it's a chance to go to the Final Four and it's not the Duke's or the Michigan State's, it's Oregon." "Fellas, when we're out there, I want to look in your eyes and see that passion and fire, now let's play." This was it, one game away from basketball immortality, the Final Four!

Neither team controlled the game's first few minutes. Both teams tested the other, and tried to identify what was going to work and what the other had scouted well enough to shut down. Freddie was a different player. We were going to need him to win, and it was clear early on that he was on top of his game. After trading baskets here and there, Kansas was on top 18-16. Then something started to happen.

Kansas was starting to score and we had stopped. Before we knew it, the score was 34-21. Kansas had blitzed us with a 16-5 run. Had we been kidding ourselves with the idea of taking on a team like Kansas? We had been able to score at will all year, especially at the right times. However, it was beginning to look like we weren't going to get out of the first half alive.

After a few substitutions, suddenly things were clicking again. Defensive stops were leading to rebounds, then to fast breaks, then to easy baskets. Freddie had scored seven straight in the midst of a 12-0 run, and, with just under three minutes left, the score was tied for the first time since 0-0. We had fought back, and avoided an early disaster, but in the final three minutes of the first half we were unable to capitalize, missing a few chances to take control of the game. At the half Kansas possessed a 48-42 lead, but as we made our way into the locker room we felt very much in the game.

"We're back in this game; we can play with these guys," Jackson said with some emotion. Several of us nodded our heads in agreement. "We've got to pick it up fellas," Rid added. Halfway through what felt like the toughest game we had played all year we were still in the game, and if we could just clean up a few of the mistakes that we had made we would have an honest shot at our highest goal.

"Well, they're forcing us to think," Coach Kent said as he walked through the locker room door. "You did a good job of weathering the storm, but we are going to have to play smarter if we want to win this game."

We all knew he was right. When you play teams of that caliber, there will be a number of runs, but ultimately it comes down to which team reaches its Breaking Point first. It had been a long time since we had reached ours, and, as we made our way from the locker room through the maze of curtains back onto the floor, the last thing we wanted to do was be the first to break.

Hoping to be the aggressor in the second half, we wanted to jump on them early forcing them to make new adjustments. However, those hopes were quickly thrown out when Kansas started right where it had finished with balanced scoring. We were able to hang on for a few minutes, but with the score 58-54; the Jayhawks went on an 8-0 scoring run and now led 66-54. Meanwhile in the crowd, Oregon quarterback Joey Harrington was trying to get the crowd back into the game. And, after a short time, he was successful. Anthony Lever had come in and provided the shooting touch that had been missing.

Behind three 3-pointers from Anthony we had gained new life with a 13-4 run and a now reachable 77-72 deficit with eight minutes to play. Freddie had continued to be outstanding, and was carrying the load with eye-candy dunks that would grab a contortionist's attention. The possibility of pulling on a Final Four T-shirt and hat after the game had again seemed realistic.

The year had been full of so many forms of success, not just as a team but also for individuals. For Freddie it was clear he had taken off the tag of inconsistency and set it on the desk of the numerous sportswriters and fence-sitting fans that were oftentimes too busy labeling growth as inconsistency. As he flew through the air for one of his dunks, I knew whatever the outcome of the game that I would certainly miss my front row seat to the high wire act of Freddie Jones!

Like so many times during the season the game would come down to getting defensive stops. If there was ever a time to put everything on the line, this was certainly it. With a loss there would be no next week, or next game, only next season.

We had started to get the defensive stops that were required, but as Kansas began missing shots, we began missing block outs. One after another Kansas was collecting rebounds. We had begun to break down, not by guarding people or the usual signs, but instead an area that hadn't been a factor all season, Rebounds!

When you give up offensive rebounds, you are giving away more than second chances. You not only erase potential offensive possessions on the other end, but usually the other team gets easy put backs or draws fouls. We were handing Kansas all of the above, compounding the problem was our inability to score. It had turned into a painful process; we would try to score, followed by them going down to the other end shooting, rebounding, shooting, and rebounding until they scored or got fouled. We felt helpless, Murphy's Law was being played out on each possession, whatever could go wrong, did!

After a 4-minute stretch without scoring, and an 87-72 deficit the last few minutes were played out as a formality. We had reached our breaking point, not

Luke Ridnour, the Ultimate floor General.

because Kansas was bigger, stronger, or more talented, but instead because we had run out of gas, failing to get stops, block out on the boards, and most importantly, failing to do the little things. Throughout the game the Jayhawks had tested and re-tested our strengths and weaknesses until they had found a way to beat us. We had been doing the same, but had failed to capitalize on any momentum we established.

Sure, they were indeed bigger, stronger and more talented, but when you can do the little things and have the heart and determination we had, you can still beat anybody.

The last few minutes were unbearable. The reality of the game was quickly setting in. You begin to realize how close you really were. Before the game it truly felt like the next big game, but as the clock was running out on our dream, the reward for winning was difficult to ignore. It wasn't so much that it was them going to the Final Four, but that it wasn't us. In a tournament where you can't afford to look ahead, we hadn't, but when the game was over, it became clear just how close we had come.

Heads were hung in both exhaustion and pure disappointment. Each player sat inconsolable on the bench. When the final horn of our game and season sounded, the result was a misleading 104-86 heartbreaking loss. It was all over. There would be no trip to Georgia the following week for the Final Four. Instead we would only get a trip back to Eugene and spring break.

GIVING THANKS ONE MORE TIME...

After shaking hands in the middle of Kansas's Final Four celebration, we found a spot on the floor, and as we had done after every game all year win or lose, we huddled up bowed our heads and together recited The Lord's Prayer. There was not only sincerity in each player's voice, but as we finished up and all eyes met, there was a sincere appreciation from one player to the other for the special ride we had shared.

On the corner of the court leading to the locker room tunnel stood Coach Kent, thanking and shaking each player's hand as he stepped off the court, some for the last time. The walk to the locker room was spent trying to convince myself that the season and my college basketball career were really over. For a game that I love and have so much passion for, this would prove more than a disappointing loss. It would be the double-edged sword. Yes, the greatest season of my short career was over, but so to was my career itself.

The locker room was tear-filled. Every player hung his head, most buried deep in their hands. The emotion of the loss was evident for more than just players. Everyone in the room could feel the pain of a wonderful run coming to an abrupt end. We had overcome so much together, growing not only as basketball players, but as friends. There would be no moral victory on this day, but in the days to follow, the sting would slowly turn to reflection on all that we had accomplished as a team.

We sat for a few minutes before Coach Kent gathered himself and walked into the locker room to deliver his final speech of the year.

Pacing around the room for a few moments he began, "It's o.k. to hurt; you're warriors, you played your tails off...it was just an incredible year and an incredible run for this institution and for yourselves."

As he choked up, Coach Kent's eyes began to water, "My tears are not because we lost, but because we don't get to play anymore, because coaches really work hard to get to this point and have teams like you guys, where all you care about is winning and you play with that inner spirit and heart."

Pausing for a few seconds to gather his thoughts and clear his throat, he finished, "Thank you again for letting us coach you. We've had a wonderful year, let's get over this hurt, go back to Eugene and start celebrating."

After he finished everyone stood preparing to team it up, "One last time, Family on three," he said. Together we repeated the word that had symbolized our team and what had made our season so special, "one… two… three… FAMILY!"

THE HURT…

After the game it was quiet for some time. Each player took his time getting up and slowly making his way out the locker room door to the family and friends who had stayed after to lend support. Like many of the other players' parents who had made the long trip, my Mom and Dad were standing just outside the tunnel. As I walked towards them, my Mom approached me, waiting for my disappointed embrace. Without having to say anything, both knew the pain that I felt. They had seen it on the faces of the players who had walked out before me and they could see it now on mine.

We stayed at the arena for about a half-hour, tying up the usual loose ends with media and family. On the bus the silence from the locker room continued. Many of the players were playing the game over and over in their heads. I could only think one thought, "I was going to miss these guys!"

Often times in the sports world you're only as good as your last game. This was not true for our game and our team. We had a great season, and although the result of our last game would be heavy on our hearts for some time, the reality of our success would last a long time!

Arriving back at the hotel, we packed, loaded the bus and were on our way back to the airport where the chartered plane awaited. In the air the mood had begun to lighten, a few laughs were heard and groups of players were huddled up talking about the parts of the game they had wished they could erase.

When the plane touched down, it felt good to be back. As the doors opened and we made the walk down the portable stairs onto the tarmac, you could see and hear people cheering on the other side of the fence. As more players deplaned, the cheers increased. We were all thinking that some of the diehards had made another trip out late at night in the cold to show their support. As we walked through the gate, there were at least 100 fans young and old. Small kids rode the shoulders of their fathers and others scrambled to get autographs of any player who passed the lines they had formed to the bus.

As we made the walk to the bus, almost every person reached a hand out and said, "thank you for such a wonderful season." The fans at the airport were just another example of the support that we had received all year. Sure, the fans can come out when you win the big games, but only six hours removed from our toughest loss of the year, they were there to thank us for giving them a wonderful season.

When the bus pulled into the Casanova Center parking lot, there was no doubt that we would see each other again, but we also knew it would no longer be the same. The wild ride of our basketball storybook season was coming to an end with the annual banquet just a few weeks away serving as the final chapter.

WHERE ONE JOURNEY ENDS ANOTHER BEGINS...

A few weeks healed some of the hurt from the disappointing loss to Kansas, but for the returning players only the following season would be closure to their continuing dream of reaching the Final Four. For the graduating players it was off on our separate paths. A few would continue playing the game we love, others including me, would take the knowledge and experience of our short lives and try and find success again.

When April 6, 2002 the night of the banquet arrived, the event had been sold out for some time. There were around 350 people in attendance, certainly record numbers. Many people had to eat in other ballrooms and watch the presentation from the halls, strange the difference a year can make. After mingling with family, friends, and fans, we sat down for the standard banquet meal that not even a great season could make taste good.

After dinner we were shown an emotional, yet jaw-dropping highlight film that had heads shaking and spines tingling. If people had forgotten one of the many Freddie dunks or Ridnour passes, the film certainly refreshed their memories. The evening concluded with awards and speeches from players and coaches. There was a great deal of emotion in the room, and, as I sat there listening to the final thoughts of players and coaches, part of me didn't want the night to end.

However this journey was over. It had been more than a success. It had been everything you dream about growing up. It was about more than winning games. It was about accomplishing something no one but ourselves believed we could accomplish.

We had revamped the record books, leaving behind an incomparable **Season of Firsts**, and in the process laid a foundation for a future where talk of national and conference championships was no longer met with laughs. It was indeed a good time to be a DUCK!

We had created a special bond that couldn't be broken by playing time, points scored, or media attention. This team wanted nothing but wins. Each loss was met with heartbreak, but also new-found knowledge. Opportunity became our personal definition for pressure where individual heroics had become an expected norm.

We defended the greatest gym in college basketball without a single blemish, something we had done with heart, courage, and a special blend of excitement unseen in the historic "PIT."

It was more than just winning the first-ever outright conference champion-ship since the Tall Firs of 1939. We had won it by two games in one of the toughest conferences in the country. We'd also blazed new trails in the NCAA tournament that will provide a measuring stick for many teams to come. But, most importantly, we built a true team full of passion, determination, sacrifice and unselfishness. Many college basketball teams will achieve the wins and accolades that come with a great year, BUT few will be able to achieve it with a rare and refreshing attitude where 15 guys are more important than one.

This team meant so much to all of us. Each person would be leaving part of himself with everyone on the team. Whether a simple memory or a lifelong friendship, this team would share more than just a basketball season together. When the banquet was finished and the majority of people had left, I began walking out to the car with my family. As my Mom put her arm around me, she said what I felt described the season in its simplest form, "This was a special year!"

For our team the road to success had been a unique and memorable journey, but for the next team April 6, 2002 marked the end of our journey and the beginning of theirs.

After all, where one journey ends another begins...

THE ACCOMPLISHMENTS AND HISTORY OF A SEASON OF FIRSTS

PAC-10 CHAMPIONS

-Oregon clinched its first outright conference championship since the 1938-39 Tall Firs, who went on to win the first NCAA Championship, won the Pacific Coast Championship… a span of 63 years.

-Overall it's the Ducks' first league crown since 1944-45, when Oregon tied for the PCC North Division title.

PAC-10 CHAMPIONS X 2

-For the first time in school history, the University of Oregon has a PAC-10 Championship in men's basketball and football in the same academic year, something that has only happened 8 times in conference history!

500-POINT CLUB

-For the first time in school history, Oregon had three players who scored 500 points in the same season. (Jones, Jackson, Ridnour)

BROKEN RECORDS

-Oregon broke seven UO single season team marks in 2001-02.
- -Points in a season
- -Sixteen 90-point games
- -School record and conference record for 3-pointers made
- -Scoring average
- -Free-throw percentage
- -Free throws made
- -Conference wins

PERFECTION

-Undefeated at home, with 16 wins, ties a school record for most home wins!

TIMELINE...FOR THE FIRST TIME

-Ever, Oregon finished the season ranked in the A.P. poll (11th)
-Ever, Oregon had six wins over top 25 teams
-Ever, Oregon scored 100 points in back-to-back league games (ASU, UA)
-In 64 years Oregon was undefeated at home
-In 57 years Oregon won 26 games
-In 27 years that Oregon was ranked in the top 10
-In 18 years that Oregon won at UCLA's Pauley Pavillion
-In 17 years that Oregon won at Arizona's McKale Center

HEAD OF THE PAC...THE DUCKS LED THE CONFERENCE IN SEVEN CATEGORIES AND RANKED IN THE TOP HALF OF 17 OF 19 OVERALL.

-Scoring Offense
-Field Goal %
-Free-throw %
-Assists
-Scoring Margin
-3-point field goal %
-3-point field goals per game

ABOUT THE AUTHOR

While at Oregon, author Ben Lindquist was a 2-time Academic All PAC-10 and 2-time winner of the University of Oregon Scholar Athlete of the Year award. Ben was a member of the Dean's List. He was the OREGON PAPE JAM MVP in 98-99 vs Minnesota. Ben was also a 3-time letter winner while at the University of Oregon. Ben played basketball at Pineview High and played one year at UVSC before moving onto Oregon.

Ben is currently a marketing consultant. He and his wife, Joy, currently reside in St. George, Utah.

For information, ordering, or suggestions on
"A Season of Firsts", log onto www.aseasonoffirsts.com.